Teaching & Learning Peace

William M. Timpson

Atwood Publishing
Madison, WI

Teaching and Learning Peace
by William M. Timpson

© Atwood Publishing, 2002

Printed in the United States of America.

ISBN: 1-891859-44-7

Atwood Publishing
2710 Atwood Ave.
Madison, WI 53704
888.242.7101
www.atwoodpublishing.com

Special thanks to the Sophia Smith Collection, Smith College, Northampton, MA
for use of photos from Anne Burlak Timpson's collected papers.

Cover design by Tamara Dever, TLC Graphics, www.tlcgraphics.com

Library of Congress Cataloging-in-Publication Data

Timpson, William M.
    Teaching and learning peace / William M. Timpson.
        p.cm.
Includes bibliographical references and index.
    ISBN 1-891859-44-7 (Paperback)
    1. Peace--Study and teaching. I. Title.
JZ5534.T56 2002
303.6'6--dc21

2002012875

TABLE OF CONTENTS

DEDICATION

To my mom, Anne Burlak Timpson, a courageous lifelong champion for peace through social justice and economic fairness.

To my wife, Gailmarie Kimmel, an equally heartfelt voice for peace through living within a simple, sustainable ethic.

And finally, to my daughter, Jayme Alissa, whose innocence about peace is sweet and clear and at eleven already a self-styled peace activist.

Acknowledgments

I must thank all those colleagues, students, and friends whose response to our teach-ins at Colorado State University following the attacks of September 11, 2001 convinced me of the importance of tapping our considerable, collective expertise on campus and in the surrounding community to better understand the root causes of that attack. Faculty from political science, history, education, speech communication, sociology, and philosophy joined with other colleagues who had direct experience in that region of the world, and with clergy from various faith-based communities in the area to share their knowledge, beliefs, fears, hopes, ideas, and ideals. In particular, I have to thank Martha Denney who was quick to offer her help in organizing these campus conversations and connecting them to the international community where Muslim students, in particular, voiced concern about their safety.

I also owe my appreciation to the first class of students in my *Teaching and Learning Peace* workshop held early in the summer of 2002. Their collective skills and training, their valuing of peace, and their deep wellspring of experiences with nonviolent alternatives added real synergy to our learning together.

In particular, fourth grade bilingual teacher and former public defender Marsha Mussehl offered wonderful insights that bridged the adversarial world of the legal system with what schools can and should do. She and eleven-year-old Jayme Alissa explored all manner of fun and creative expressions of peacemaking during the week. Marsha also provided wonderful feedback on the entire manuscript.

My thanks to our guest speakers for the week: To my colleague Nat Kees whose meditations set a tone of socially conscious mindfulness; to Grace Marie whose Dances for Universal Peace inspired deeper connections to heart and soul; to Roe Bubar whose work with Native American peoples helped us honor the past while we explored possibilities for a better future; to Charlotte Miller from the Quaker Society of Friends and Dayna Ring from the Bahaists (their faith-based commitments to nonviolence, communication, and acceptance stand as powerful models of peaceful possibilities); to Tom Cavanagh whose work for restorative justice challenges conventional thinking about punishment and offers a very new paradigm for healing. And a special thanks to my colleague, Barbara Gotshall, whose heartfelt interest in peace helped to spark this first workshop.

As always, I am indebted for the encouragement and support I receive from friends and family members who share my hopes for a better world. I must also acknowledge the leadership of President Al Yates of Colorado State University in articulating renewed attention to civility and values, as well as the support I receive from the Provost's office for my work with the Center for Teaching and Learning. Jeanne Clarke, Administrative Assistant for the Center, is a constant source of help as I fit my writing in with everything else we do on campus.

And finally, to Linda Babler at Atwood Publishing, who shares my commitment to peacemaking and social justice as well as my hope that this book will inspire others.

PREFACE

The names Gandhi, King, Mandela, Boulding, and Hanh are known far and wide as champions of peace through nonviolence. There is also a rich literature on teaching and learning, from kindergarten through high school and on into college and university. My hope for this book is to connect what we know about peacemaking to what we know about communication and cooperation in classrooms, about anger management and emotional intelligence, about critical and creative thinking. Although my own writing now centers on post-secondary instruction, I also taught at the junior and senior high school levels in the inner city of Cleveland; and, for the past thirty years, I have continued to work closely with K-12 teachers. Given the impact of the attacks of September 11, 2001, this book should have relevance for educators, church and community leaders everywhere as they explore what kinds of constructive roles they can play in teaching peace and helping others learn alternatives to violence.

The "students" who joined me for our very first workshop on *Teaching and Learning Peace*, in the summer of 2002 represented a diverse audience. Our guest speakers added to that diversity and confirmed for me the value of making this connection between peacemaking, teaching, and learning. We had a fourth grade teacher as well as an elementary school counselor, a former social worker, a university professor, a Presbyterian minister, and a community activist as well as an eleven year old "peace activist."

We also had several individuals with extensive overseas experiences, including a Vietnam veteran. One person had made trips to the then USSR and China in the 1980s as part of a citizen initiative to help build understanding and reverse the nuclear arms build up. Another has been involved with reconciliation work in Rwanda after the genocidal wars there. Yet another lived in the Philippines and witnessed U.S. efforts to negotiate a nonviolent transition when it was threatened by revolution toward the end of the Marcos regime. We also had a university administrator who wanted to help focus campus expertise on this issue of peacemaking.

Between our guest speakers and our workshop members, we had several people who had direct experience with the destructive impact of violence here in our own country. They could see the relevance of an emphasis on peacemaking at every level and in every context — from fighting in schools to violence in homes, from the violence that can be done to an individual's psyche by being abandoned to the self destructive violence that comes from drug and alcohol abuse.

As such, I think this book should have wide appeal. Teachers and counselors in elementary and secondary schools will appreciate a approach that links anger management, for example, to deeper issues of peace and nonviolence, and puts them in a context of theories that have proven effective and practical. College and university instructors across the various disciplines will appreciate the links between course design, classroom functioning, and the inculcation of skills and attitudes that can deepen learning through greater cooperation and better conflict resolution — all within a context that links peace and nonviolence with social justice and environmental responsibility. Civility and character development are just two of the more recent emphases in higher education that relate to the teaching and learning of peace. Church leaders and community activists will also appreciate these interconnections.

Introduction

How do we teach about peace? How do we help young people manage their own anger and aggressiveness when violence is so prevalent in their lives, at school and on the streets, in the news, on television, in the movies, and in the lyrics of some of their music? When memories of attacks are raw and calls for retaliation are shrill, how does an educator — or anyone in a leadership role who is committed to the ideals of a sustainable peace — open a meaningful dialogue about alternatives to violence? At its core, democracy demands open and honest discussions and we can do much in our schools, colleges, and universities to support responsible citizenship.

Dictators rule without question, their weaknesses sheltered by brute force, nepotism, terror, and the like. In a search for peace, however, we have many heroes to call on for inspiration and guidance. Some like Gandhi, Martin Luther King Jr., Thich Nhat Hanh, Elise Boulding, and Nelson Mandela are well known. Others are less public but come from communities like the Quaker Society of Friends, the Mennonites, and the Bahaists, who share a core religious belief in peace and nonviolence. Some like Dorothy Day dedicated their church work to social justice, hunger, and the poor.

My own heroes also include my mother. She had to leave school after the ninth grade to work in the nearby textile mills and help support her family. She quickly received a baptism by fire into the all too often brutal world of corporate greed in the 1920s, when bosses were intent on keeping wages low, their own profits high, and unions out of their plants. She was arrested many times. By the age of eighteen, my mom had already been fired for "talking union" (fair pay and decent conditions) at two mills nearby her birth town in Bethlehem, Pennsylvania. On her very first job, she was offered $9 for a fifty-two hour work week while boys got $12 for the same job. Already gifted with the courage to speak out, she wanted to know why. The burly company man said so very condescendingly, "Girlie, boys need more money. If you don't want the job, others do."

The shock of that experience, however, paled in comparison to her very first opportunity to speak in public. The year was 1929. Though still a teenager, she was already a veteran of the labor movement. On this memorable day in May, she joined with fifteen or so others to protest a local ban on public gatherings, put in place to quell rumbling worker unrest over brutal conditions at the Bethlehem Steel plant — twelve hour work days, six day work weeks, low pay, unsafe conditions, company houses, stores with exorbitant prices, and on and on. Keeping order and keeping dissent down was absolutely necessary for company profit margins to remain high and the local elite secure in their privilege. The local police, of course, were there to enforce "order." As my mom wrote (Timpson, 2002):

> We came with a group of some fifteen people to the designated corner and quickly set up a portable platform. We draped an American flag in front of it, and I mounted the platform. I stated that the International Labor Defense was an organization that defended workers who were struggling for their rights as American citizens, and I wanted to tell them of these rights. I then started to read from the Bill of Rights. "Congress shall make no law...abridging the freedom of speech, or of the press, or the right of the people peaceably to assemble and to petition the Government for a redress of grievances...." I got no further. Two mounted police came thundering towards me, as workers coming out of Bethlehem Steel stared. One policeman dismounted and yanked me off the platform, while the other held his horse. I

tried to continue to read the Bill of Rights, but the cop slapped me right across my mouth, while the young people around me cried "Free speech, free speech."

My dad was schooled by the hard times of the Great Depression in these same concerns for economic fairness and social justice. Early on he helped to organize dairy farmers in Wisconsin who saw their chance for a better life undermined by milk producers taking most of the profits. Like my mom, he learned to speak out at a young age and in the face of real danger. He went on to volunteer to fight in two different wars against fascism. In 1936 he volunteered for the John Brown artillery battery of the International Brigade to fight for the elected Republican forces against the rebellion led by the fascist General Franco. Idealism had to be high because the equipment was poor and the casualties were staggering. Despite an international embargo that only hampered the Republican forces, Hitler and Mussolini supplied arms, troops, airplanes, and more to Franco's forces. Picasso's famous *Guernica* commemorates the devastation from experiments with carpet bombing of heavily populated urban areas. Surviving this Spanish Civil War my dad returned home only to volunteer after Pearl Harbor again and fight with Patton's U.S. Third Army from D-Day across southern France and into Germany.

Once back in Boston where I was born and raised, my father worked as a "sandhog," a tunnel worker, wielding those deafening jackhammers and moving dirt for sewers, foundations, highways, and car tunnels. The constant dust led to his own early death from emphysema. Although he had two years of college and then two years of teaching in a one room school back in Wisconsin, he always identified politically with the working man, the proletariat, the hero of leftist ideologies. That is, until 1956 when the paranoid brutality of Stalin became public and the dream of a proletariat-led stateless utopia was shattered for him. My father felt betrayed and his sacrifices in two wars compromised.

The tensions of the Cold War became seismic in our home. The McCarthy hysteria seemed to put my mom, in particular, under a public microscope. Suddenly, all those battles to improve conditions for textile workers were painted bright red as paranoia swept the country. Because of all that, my parents chose to rent in the Roxbury section of Boston, once heavily Jewish and then predominantly African American. There we

Art Timpson before leaving for Spain.
Reprinted with permission from the Sophia
Smith Collection, Smith College,
Northampton, MA.

would be somewhat shielded from public persecution since the historic racism of that city and the clarity of my parents' opposition to oppression of all sorts made us, for the most part, welcomed.

Growing up in that environment meant an easy identification for me and my sister with the goals of the emerging Civil Rights movement. Domestic "peace" for people of color meant a desire for America to live up to its own ideals, its Declaration of Independence, and its Constitution. Justice was always something you had to fight for, sing for, petition and march for. While I battled the self-consciousness common to every adolescent's development, I still saw my parents speaking out whenever and wherever injustice appeared. School, however, was important and especially the study of history and economics. My parents had been convinced, like so many others during those dark days of the Great Depression, that there was an inevitability, a determinism to be unlocked through study of those disciplines, in particular. Political debates dominated our household, from the macro and theoretical to the micro and strategic.

Coming of draft age just as the Vietnam War heated up, I lived through the shift in focus from civil rights at home to questioning the very morality of a war so far away. Protests and marches put dissent into the streets and politicians on call. I was now teaching math, social studies, and literacy in the inner city of Cleveland, Ohio where I had a deferment from the draft for two years.

Through all this, a lifelong joy in learning drew me toward education. Looking back I could see how quickly I slid into a teaching role at an early age, volunteering to coach a Pee Wee baseball team when I myself was playing in the Little League. Going to the YMCA all those years after school led, at a later time, to coaching younger kids in basketball and other sports. Playing football in high school meant developing a certain toughness and stoicism, however, although I also kept a degree of curiosity about our defensive systems and offensive blocking assignments. That all changed when I was dressed out in front of the entire team by the line coach for "asking too many damn questions."

Anne Burlak Timpson with Bill and Kat after her release from prison. Reprinted with permission from the Sophia Smith Collection, Smith College, Northampton, MA.

While the Vietnam war raged overseas, protests were heating up at home. Cleveland was one of the first cities to explode in unrest. The Glennville riot produced a dozen or so deaths as gun battles raged and the burning began. Just when I thought I was missing the war overseas, something like it exploded all around me. National Guard troops were patrolling the streets near Patrick Henry Junior High School. The Junior Black Panthers were marching in front of the school. Behind every door, pine paddles were employed to help keep order. Some preferred finely tooled and stained oak paddles with leather wrist straps that they could commission in the wood shop. Half inch holes meant less "wind resistance" and "greater impact." Corporal punishment was widely supported among parents who saw danger in the streets and wanted their own children to have a safe environment in school, the one arena that held out hope for escaping the ghetto. I look back and wonder about the relationship between the violence used to keep order in school (and often at home) and the violence that threatened that order in the first place.

While Cleveland simmered, marches against the war drew me and thousands of others to demonstrations in Washington. Something electric was in the air, as the normally staid Howard Johnson restaurants on the highways leading to the nation's capitol were suddenly bustling with kids my age replete in their costumes of jeans, tie-dyes and bandanas. The way in which Nixon used National Guard vehicles to ring the White House spoke volumes to us about the power of mass demonstrations, lessons passed on to me from an earlier time by my parents.

In the midst of those storms, graduate school at the University of Wisconsin from 1972-1976 meant relative quiet. A few lingering protests periodically stirred Madison — the counter march mourning Nixon's inauguration, the annual Mifflin Street block parties that often got out of hand and meant a trashing of State Street. Yet, there was a strange unease for me on that campus. Way too much theory and way too much rhetorical sparring for this son of working class activists.

Nearing completion of my Ph.D. in educational psychology, I took a position at Colorado State University. In contrast to Wisconsin, Colorado is a much more conservative state. I was used to cities and states dominated by the Democratic Party and a more liberal agenda. Colorado felt like alien territory to me, with its historic Republican majorities and the vocal presence of gun lobbies and religious fundamentalists. Yet, my work directing a Teacher Corps Project kept me connected to the poor and predominantly Hispanic communities in the north of the state as well as to Native American communities in the region. I could see how local unrest was connected to a sense of historic injustice and economic unfairness. Education offered hope for something better; that is, until Ronald Reagan pulled the plug.

Fortunately, a Kellogg National Fellowship from 1981 to 1984 helped me stay connected with the wider world, its conflicts and the roles that teachers could play. The Fellowship allowed me to travel widely in China, Hong Kong,0 and Taiwan. I saw how historic disputes festered just under the surface, often bubbling up into the schools as the old order of British imperialism faded from the scene. The Cultural Revolution in China, under Mao's reign in the 1960s, saw the Red Guard persecute and brutalize teachers.

I also got to travel to Brazil to see the impact of Paulo Freire's work for national literacy there as well as in Cuba and Nicaragua. North of Managua I talked to teachers who routinely had to bury their books lest the U.S. backed Contras find them and execute all those involved as "representatives" of the Sandinista government. Learning to read was clearly a subversive act in those times. In Havana I visited a museum dedicated to the literacy campaign and saw photographs, for example, of the elderly being outfitted with glasses for the first time in their lives and making those very first steps toward reading and entry into the modern world. Advances in health care in these countries were dependent on an increase in literacy. Dysentery, for example, could be reduced dramatically if people could read about the importance of boiling water.

The build-up to the Gulf War put everyone on alert. Appreciative of our country's commitment to work through the United Nations, I still agonized over the loss of life on the Iraqi side. Here for the first time I could see direct daily evidence of the devastating impact of war on the environment. Everyone seemed touched by images of so many deliberately set oil well fires and the abandoned hulks of Iraqi tanks littering highways. There was a real fear of a new age of biological weapons in the hands of people we did not trust. Certain questions kept haunting me: Just what is the relationship between education and warfare, between science and new forms of weapons, between the powerful and the weak?

Genocide in Rwanda and ethnic cleansing in the Balkans raised questions about intervention far from home even for the most noble of reasons. Debates swirled over the limits of U.S. power and influence, its superpower status and a possible role as a "world cop." Discussions also emerged over the political viability of strategic military interventions, primarily from the air, where U.S. casualties — and consequently, political criticism at home — would be minimized.

And then came the attacks of September 11, 2001. In my large lecture class of first year students that morning, I made some general and very personal comments about my own shock and grief, about the importance of understanding what happened, of using what we had been learning to reflect on our feelings, consider various options and think long term about what would be needed for a sustainable peace in such a volatile, war ravaged area of the world. I played a song from *Sweet Honey and the Rock,* an African American acappella group dedicated to social justice and peace. Their original song — *I Remember, I Believe* — bravely describes how faith endures despite tragedies and suffering all around.

I then opened up the floor for anyone to comment. One of our section leaders warned against overreacting and attacking Muslims here at home. A student also spoke up about tolerance. The 150 or so other students in attendance, however, were silent, numbed by the events of that morning. I began to connect the readings for that week on Transactional Analysis to the possibility of understanding terror and anger, how the rebellious "child" in any person can give vent to rage and go on the attack, and how educated people everywhere needed to access their "adult" capabilities to mediate raw emotion and draw on their wisdom to find alternatives to violence. Class ended and we all went our own ways.

Since the attacks we have also seen a dramatic upsurge of violence in the Middle East with suicide bombings and military reprisals in a seemingly endless display of retaliation. The historic tensions in Northern Ireland have also flared periodically. As Gandhi once said, "An eye for an eye and a tooth for a tooth leaves everyone blind and toothless." Yet I was encouraged by hearing from Nelson Mandela in the summer of 2001 at a conference in South Africa about the importance of our work in higher education for defining a just, fair, and prosperous future. I was then reminded of the urgency of our working for peace and nonviolent conflict resolution by a tour through Eastern Europe in the summer of 2002 when I saw first hand the legacy of World War II, the holocaust, and Soviet occupation.

So how does it stop? What constructive role can we play, especially those of us in education or other leadership positions. For me, the ideas and skills laid out in this text provide one way forward, connecting the importance of nonviolence with the skills of mediation and some understanding of creative conflict resolution. As depicted in the brilliant film, *An Everlasting Peace,* an Irish Catholic and a Protestant find common ground to make a first gesture toward ending the violence all around. I too search for hope in the midst of despair, for some light in the darkness by connecting teaching and learning with peacemaking.

Part I: Laying the Groundwork

As instructors, we can insist on the kinds of processes that support an exploration of peaceful alternatives to conflict. To do so we should frequently point out and examine how behavior on the national and international level is parallel to or gets its beginnings from individual and classroom behavior. We lay the groundwork by pointing out where violent behavior originates and offering alternatives on a level familiar to both teachers and students.

The chapters in Part I offer practical approaches to understanding how such things as the desire for revenge manifest themselves on both the world stage and in the classroom.

Chapter 1

RETHINKING REVENGE

In his autobiography, *Long Walk to Freedom*, Nelson Mandela (1994) argues for a vision that can help keep us free from the bitter desire for revenge when we have been wronged or feel persecuted, a motivation that too often leads to an escalation of violence and reprisal. Imprisoned for twenty-seven years on Robben Island for his ceaseless work against apartheid — a system of brutal subjugation of the black majority by a privileged white minority — Mandela had every reason to be consumed by anger. Instead he pushed himself and those around him to identify a higher ground outside that *prison* of oppression and reprisal.

> Freedom is indivisible; the chains on any one of my people were the chains on all of them, the chains on all of my people were the chains on me. It was during those long and lonely years that my hunger for the freedom of my own people became a hunger for the freedom of all people, white and black. I knew it as well as I knew anything that the oppressor must be liberated just as surely as the oppressed. A man who takes away another man's freedom is a prisoner of hatred, he is locked behind the bars of prejudice and narrow-mindedness. I

am not truly free if I am taking away someone else's freedom, just as surely as I am not free when my freedom is taken away from me. The oppressed and the oppressor alike are robbed of their humanity. (1994, 624)

So often the violence needed to sustain oppression only induces a round of violence in response. In our classrooms, we can help students see the interconnectedness among all peoples, between their own privileges, for example, and the sacrifices of those who have had to make do with much less. We can help students recognize the sources of prejudice that lurk in the unexamined crevices of their own psyches. We can help them help others rethink their biases.

One of the real joys of learning is the flash of insight when something first makes sense, when you break through "conventional wisdom" and see a creative new possibility. Thomas Kuhn's (1970) classic, *The Structure of Scientific Revolutions* describes the process by which the prevailing paradigms that define our thinking gradually give way to new models as counter-evidence grows. Galileo was persecuted as a heretic when he dared to suggest that the earth was not the center of the universe. In some areas of the U.S. the word "evolution" has been purged from science texts as creationists push to have their interpretation dominate.

I had such a shift in thinking when I first read Maurice Friedman's (2000) description of the Hasidic Jewish interpretation of the Old Testament ethic of *"an eye for an eye."* I had always understood that idea as a moral argument in defense of revenge and a major barrier to healing, forgiveness, and peace. In areas where groups come into conflict, it is easy to see how the combatants on both sides who adhere to this scripture could get locked into a bitter and bloody pursuit of revenge. Just who would have the last killing? Friedman, however, puts a different spin on it.

> What is unique in the Hasidic approach to reconciliation is that it points the way to seeing justice and love as necessary complements of each other rather than as alternatives between which one must choose....The large majority of people in our culture hold the distorted view that the God of the Old Testament is a harsh and wrathful God in contrast to the loving and merciful God of the New....An "eye for an eye and a tooth for a tooth" is *not* the expression of a vengeful God but a primitive statement of

basic social democracy in which no [one] is held of greater worth than another, because each is created in the image of God....Throughout all history, indeed, the natural *inequality* of man has justified razing a whole city to revenge the murder of one privileged man. Countless others have been exterminated with impunity because they were slaves or serfs or members of an "inferior race." "An eye for an eye" is a fundamental conception of social justice. (2000, 119)

In other words, some who are bent on revenge have long rationalized their actions through their interpretation of these lines from the scripture. I also assumed that loyalty to Old Testament teachings locked the faithful into a vengeful mindset. However, I now see that there are alternate interpretations of those very same lines I once saw as problematic. On the world stage, it could be that unprovoked attacks on civilian targets like the one of September 11 keep too many of us mired in violence as the *only* choice of responses, one that we can justify with the Old Testament code of an "eye for an eye."

In the classroom, we may have to point out the need to reassess beliefs and stay committed to what is life affirming. For example, we can examine instances where any of us has felt hurt by a particular comment and lashed back in anger. Naming the underlying motivation can go far toward helping students unpack the dangers inherent in revenge and move toward alternative responses. Some students vie for attention. Others want control. A few may feel helpless much of the time. The work of Dreikurs (1968), in particular, offers useful ideas for understanding how these motivations can play out and what options instructors have.

Dreikurs hypothesizes the following relationships between a student's inner motivation or goals and the feelings evoked in others. Knowing about these motivations and responses can provide a useful tool for intervening when conflicts arise and revenge rears its ugly head.

- Someone seeking *revenge* for something in the past can produce feelings of hurt in others; dealing with emotions openly and sensitively can help a group, and an individual, move on.

- Someone seeking *power* will typically produce feelings of competitiveness in others; periodic reminders about cooperation may help.

- Someone seeking *attention* will often generate feelings of annoyance in others. Naming the behavior for what it is can help students identify the source of their frustration and address the issue in a constructive manner. For example, group members could agree to a ground rule that maximizes participation, that allows everyone a chance to speak before any one individual gets to speak a second time.

- Someone acting *helpless* can engender feelings of inadequacy in others. When some people just can't get an idea, it may be best to get others involved, to point students toward other resources on campus.

Revenge may not be the only excuse for violence, but it has been important historically, especially with respect to individual motivation. In teaching and learning peace, we can always analyze a situation before violence erupts.

Chapter 2

Understanding Creativity & Conceptual Thinking

Mairead Corrigan Maguire (2000) was the winner of the 1977 Nobel Peace Prize for her work in Northern Ireland involving ordinary people in the effort to end the historic violence there and build a culture of peace. When addressing these kinds of complex issues, with all their systemic reasons and historic roots, she notes Gandhi's insistence that "nonviolence does not mean passivity. It is the most daring, creative, and courageous way of living, and it is the only hope for the world. Nonviolence demands creativity" (p. 161). In Maquire's outline for a sustainable peace, you can see just how daunting the challenge really is. In the comments that follow, she offers recommendations that can help students begin thinking creatively about the active dimensions of nonviolence.

> Fifty years after his death, Gandhi challenges us to pursue a new millennium of nonviolence. This is not an impossible dream. First, we need to teach nonviolence....Second, as individuals, we can exorcize the violence and untruth from our own lives. We can stop supporting systemic violence and militarism, and dedicate ourselves to nonviolent social change. We

can take public stands for disarmament and justice, and take new risks for peace. Third, we can urge the media to stop sensationalizing violence and instead to highlight peaceful interactions, promote nonviolence, and uphold those who strive for peace. Fourth, we can embrace the wisdom of nonviolence that lies underneath each of the world's religions....The world's religions need to come together in dialogue and respect, because there can be no world peace until the great religions make peace with one another....Fifth, we need to pursue Gandhi's dream of unarmed, international peacemaking teams which resolve international conflict....Perhaps the greatest contribution we can pay to Gandhi is to work to eliminate poverty from the face of the earth. Gandhi said that poverty is the worst form of violence. (2000, 161-162)

To help students consider the importance of nonviolent alternatives at every level, encourage them to explore the creative process. Most people have some intuitive feel for what's creative. We can think about it as innovation or insight, new ideas or possibilities, "thinking outside the box," or "pushing the envelope." Although we may be able to see creativity in others, we may not know much about cultivating our own creative potential. If you believe people like Maguire, creativity becomes especially important for promoting peace in the midst of conflict. If you believe the futurists, creativity will become increasingly valuable as computers and technology continue to expand into every aspect of our work and personal lives, freeing us up to explore, design, and create new possibilities for old problems.

The question is, how do we best use our creativity? As a nation we can, for example, continue to put vast resources and creative energies into research on new weapons systems and our capacity for war generally or we can begin to insist on new mechanisms for peace. The U.S. currently spends $100 million dollars a day just maintaining its nuclear arsenal. Our annual military expenditures are more than the sum of the annual military expenditures for the next fifteen countries combined. We have a cabinet level Department of Defense as well as three military academies. When do we get a Department of Peace and at least one "peace academy?"

Paradoxically, the ability to think in new ways can become increasingly difficult for young people as they move through their formal schooling. Despite their natural curiosity and drive for independence, students spend many years in formal classroom settings where they are taught to follow certain rules, master particular skills, regurgitate known "facts," and hypothesize about various theories. How much of their innate inquisitiveness and spontaneity, for example, gets stifled or lost because of this kind of prescribed learning? If you become very proficient at jumping over educational hurdles, do you run the risk of losing sight of the journey your inner self wants to make? Remember the famous Robert Frost poem about the "path less taken" and how "that made all the difference"? Addressing these kinds of questions is at the heart of the creative process.

But what defines creativity? What do we know about it? Can we recognize it? Can we teach it and how? Patrick's (1955) identification of the stages of creativity has proven useful as a starting point. The first stage is *preparation*, where you collect data and resources. Because of the very nature of creativity, however, how you prepare may be open to question. If you really do want a fresh look at an old problem, what data do you look at and what resources do you collect? When you take on some project for peacemaking, for example, you will need enough time to talk about your ideas and get lots of input, to read widely, to explore resources in the library, on the Web or in the community, to consult with others, etc. Early in this process, you will want to be active and organized but consciously uncommitted to any specific outcome, open to different perspectives and new insights.

According to Patrick, the second stage involves *incubation*, where you dwell on various ideas and possibilities, some of which may seem quite far fetched, without a focused (or even conscious) attention to any one particular solution. You have to let ideas percolate, and then be alert to what bubbles up. Know that this process can take considerable time and cause frustration. However, just knowing about the role of incubation can help you better plan and manage this aspect of the creative process.

The third stage involves *illumination,* or what has been called the *Ah-ha!* phenomenon, when a solution may suddenly spring to mind. Whenever you feel stuck with nothing new coming to mind, you have to trust this stage in the creative process and wait. You never know when a flash of insight will happen. Useful ideas often arise when people are doing something else.

A fourth and final stage requires *verification*, when you assess the implications of your insights and conduct any additional experiments as tests of your ideas. Not all creative insights will be useful. Some might be absurd. Use this stage to assess whatever surfaces.

Now return to the challenges set out by Maguire. How can Patrick's stages help us think about teaching nonviolence or ridding our own psyches of its influence, about changing the focus of our media and celebrating peacemakers, about addressing poverty and racism as fundamental sources of conflict? Understanding more about creativity can provide much needed patience and wisdom. At the American Educational Research Association's annual conferences, the Special Interest Group on Peace Education has often featured speakers from Northern Ireland. I have been impressed with the mix of resourcefulness and perseverance in their efforts to end the violence in that long-suffering land. Schools, for example, have been the site for trying new approaches to nurture peacemaking.

EXPLORERS, ARTISTS, JUDGES, AND WARRIORS

Roger von Oech (1986) has a delightful book titled, *A Kick in the Seat of the Pants,* in which he hypothesized four essential roles in the creative process. The *explorer,* the *artist,* the *judge,* and the *warrior* represent qualities that underlie innovation. Anyone of us, insists von Oech, can develop our own creative potential by nurturing these qualities in ourselves, by putting on these different "hats" and "costumes."

The *explorer* in us can take risks and venture forth into the unknown of peacemaking. In the summer of 2002, my workshop, *Teaching and Learning Peace,* led directly to the writing of this book. Despite a short timeline, other responsibilities and deadlines, a spirit of adventure fueled my work. I wasn't sure I could pull it all together, but it seemed to be the right thing to do, a contribution to peacemaking I had made a promise to myself to complete after the attacks of September 11, 2001.

The *artist* in us can also bring some aesthetic appreciation to this work for nonviolence, giving us intuitive insight and another perspective. Years ago I got to visit the Children's Peace Memorial in Hiroshima, Japan. Every year, schoolchildren from all over the country bring their paper chains of origami peace cranes to dress this statue. Instead of a stoic testimonial, this statue has an engaging and enduring vitality to it, brilliantly colorful and ever changing, but requiring the attention and effort of many schools, teachers, and students every year to sustain.

The *judge* in us can be both analytical and decisive. As an example, in the days after the attacks on September 11, a few of us on campus worked to organize two teach-ins. We had to make a lot of decisions in a very short amount of time — who to invite, where and when to host the event, how to advertise. The situation demanded a quick turnaround time in order to be effective.

The *warrior* in us can go out in the world and make things happen, sometimes, however, at some risk. There were a few criticisms of various speakers during our teach-ins. In a public forum, with complex issues that evoke strong feelings, would you expect anything else? In von Oech's language, the *warrior's* spirit allowed us to persevere and celebrate this kind of peaceful engagement, no matter how emotional. Nearly everyone with whom I talked, and especially the students, seemed to appreciate the opportunity to understand more about the background to the attacks and to hear from people with different backgrounds, beliefs, and values.

Another example becomes useful here, a bittersweet story about creative solutions under threat in a complex world. Reclaimed vacant lots in New York City that once were eyesores and dumps had been cleaned up by volunteers in the neighborhood and planted with vegetables and trees. Here was a local, creative, community-based and life-affirming solution to neglected and often dangerous areas. Suddenly there was a place and a reason for city folks and gardeners to come together. But then came the violence of bulldozers as developers pushed to make way for the construction of new housing (Bruinius, 1999). As this story unfolds, you can see the stages of creativity as well as the roles that were played out.

> For decades, many urban communities have cleaned up abandoned garbage-filled lots and planted gardens — often with the cities' encouragement — in an effort to improve their neighborhoods. As the economy thrives, however, these city-owned lots are now prime targets for development....So far, 44 gardens have been bulldozed....The city plans to auction 112 more in May, as part of an effort to sell some of its 11,000 vacant lots. It contends the land is needed to build

affordable housing. But many community activists find it ironic that the work neighbors did to improve their communities and increase the value of the land is one reason the gardens are threatened....

Community gardens began blooming in big cities in the 1960s and '70s as a result of the civil rights movement and its effort to find ways to improve decaying urban areas.....The city contends gardeners knew from the start use of the land was temporary....But activists like David Crane say there are plenty of other parcels the city could use....

On the block surrounding the lot where the Garden of Love used to be, 11 tenement buildings stand empty, their arched windows and ornate doorways boarded up....At the space where (local teacher and gardener) Goodridge and his students used to plant trees and listen to stories, a new, shiny chain-link fence now encloses the empty lot. Bricks jut out of the rocky soil still marked by bulldozer tracks, and garbage is already beginning to gather. 'The fence says they won't be building anything here soon,' says Goodrich. (1999, 2,4)

You can see signs of the roles described by von Oech in this story. Facing empty, trashed-out lots where drug dealing and violence were often spawned, these neighbors called on their own talents and energies for a creative solution. On your own campus, is the idea of a garden viable, a place to raise fresh vegetables? Do you find the idea attractive? (You may need your *artist's* hat to answer that.) Can you *explore* the possibility of converting unused land into garden space? Would others get excited about that kind of possibility? Would this issue resonate with student idealism about a better world and about putting theories into practice? How could you find out? Here you will need your analytical *judge's* hat. Along with the food you could grow, what are the other savings you could get by converting grassy areas which require water, chemical fertilizers, pesticides, and weed control herbicides as well as human and other resources to mow and maintain? Do you like this idea enough to put your *warrior* into action? Becoming alert to the "violence" we commit on our own campus spaces may help link awareness to conflicts far away. Lessons learned in using our creative talents locally may help develop the skills we need for peacemaking elsewhere.

Mental Traps

In *The Ecology of Commerce,* Paul Hawken (1994) challenges traditional thinking about the relationship between economic productivity and the environment, and between the ignorance and selfish consumerism that underlies inequities worldwide, so often the source of conflicts and war.

> Gasoline is cheap in the United States because its price does not reflect the cost of smog, acid rain, and their subsequent effects on health and the environment. Likewise, American food is the cheapest in the world, but the price does not reflect the fact that we have depleted the soil, reducing average topsoil from a depth of twenty-one to six inches over the past hundred years, contaminated our groundwater (farmers do not drink from wells in Iowa), and poisoned wildlife through the use of pesticides. When prices drop, effectively raising real income, people don't need to think about waste, frugality, product life cycles, or product substitution. When prices rise, people have to reconsider usage patterns. This may be painful at first, but it generally results in innovation and creativity. (1994, 76)

So what do we do? If Hawken is right, how do we avoid falling into guilt and despair over these enduring realities? Do we become paralyzed, defensive of our lifestyles and choices but in denial about real solutions? How do we get to innovative alternatives? Are too many of us locked into one way of thinking, addicted to our own "stuff," our cars and disposables, unable to see other possibilities, unwilling to rethink our assumptions, beliefs, values, and behaviors? Does a sustainable peace require this level of soul searching?

In *A Whack on the Side of the Head*, Roger von Oech (1983) describes the creative process itself, the "locks" that confine our minds and how each of us can increase our own inventiveness. If we think through von Oech's "locks" and the challenge from Hawken quoted above, we may be able to see places where we have gotten trapped by our thinking.

Mental lock #1: The insistence on the "right" answer

It's a natural, developmental process to think about what's right. Perry (1999) refers to this as *dichotomous thinking,* where "truth" is objective, externally determined by research and authorities, textbooks and teachers. But look at the ongoing debates that swirl around our response to various conflicts and what the impact will be on our own economy. "Experts" line up on all sides of any issue, loudly proclaiming the truthfulness of their solutions. Who's "right?" What might be "true" about each position? Is a polarized debate useful? How can we learn from each other?

As Perry argues, intellectual maturation requires a growing ability to handle complexity and ambiguity, to sort through various arguments, to examine the data available and know when to seek further evidence, to ask questions and stay open to possibilities while developing an internal self-confidence or *agency*. Is there one right answer to the picture which Hawken paints, our inability to assign appropriate costs to the market's depletion of the environment? Is there an important economic lesson from the attacks on September 11, for example that we cannot abandon a military ally and its war torn landscape to the ravages of poverty and warlord chaos? Or do we need to begin to think in some very new ways?

Mental lock #2: A preoccupation with what is assumed to be logical

If you listen to advocates for the free market, you will hear all the reasons why tinkering with the economy will only cause problems, e.g., artificial manipulation of interest rates, the subsidy of various practices, or the imposition of protective tariffs. You'll see all their graphs, charts, and formulas, and you'll hear all their stories from the past where people wandered from the fold of marketplace orthodoxy. They'll also leave you with the "only" logical conclusion that they must be RIGHT! But wait, cautions von Oech. Are we making some faulty assumptions here? Are we using suspect logic? Are there are other ways to think? For instance, can we have a more "intelligent" market economy if we factor in the costs to the environment from pollution or from using our military forces to protect our "national interests" around the globe, formulas which might decrease our wastefulness and reduce the risk of bloodshed?

Mental lock #3: A conforming impulse to follow the rules

Why do we follow rules in the first place? Part of the problem may be our own place in the hierarchy, our need for employment, to fit into some corporate or organizational culture. Too many of us may be following conventional rules and therefore blinded from seeing other possibilities. Lawrence Kohlberg (1963) refers to mindless "obedience" as the lowest stage of moral thinking. Given Hawken's example about accumulating environmental damage, we might find new ideas in more activist groups like Greenpeace and Earthfirst. Nonviolent civil disobedience has a long and storied history among peacemakers. If Hawken is right and the problem is largely us and how we do business, when do we begin to get creative about the rules we live by?

MENTAL LOCK #4: THE CALL FOR PRACTICALITY

Have you ever used the phrase, "Let's be practical"? What does that really mean? Do you ever find yourself dismissing some ideas because you're convinced that "they just won't work"? And then you find out you were wrong? In later chapters of his book, Hawken describes businesses that have adopted environmentally sustainable principles and succeeded, something that may originally have been dismissed as impractical. One example is of a carpet company, *Interweave,* which developed a system of sectional design so that a small soiled area could be replaced without ripping out an entire room and dumping a lot of perfectly good carpet into a landfill. Thinking more sustainably about the environment may help us develop a broader, more enduring vision for peace.

MENTAL LOCK #5: THE PRESSURES TO STAY ON TASK

What happened in your classes or meetings immediately after the September 11 attacks? Did you break stride from the scheduled content coverage? Some instructors seem so focused on getting through their material that they lose sight of those students who have questions or might need to talk. Should instructors continue when students have lost interest, need a break, or something different to renew their energies? Do you know people, good-minded and concerned but so busy with their work that they have no time or energy for anything else? Under pressure to stay competitive, can we become so efficient and so focused on our next step that we miss various warning signs all around us? Should we address "teachable moments" that go beyond the narrow definitions of our course content areas and our own expertise?

Mental lock #6: The avoidance of ambiguity

In their orientation toward correct answers, reinforced by years of formal schooling, students can become quite impatient with ambiguity and discussions about complex issues, for example. The benefit of hindsight can be illuminating when we read through the following excerpt from Godfrey Sperling's reflections on Vice President Al Gore's presidential chances in early 1999. It is interesting to hear a well-published commentator confess his uncertainty and admit to the difficulty of working within so much ambiguity. This analysis becomes so much more important given the attacks of September 11 and the President's responses thereafter.

> Politics is so hard to explain. That's partly what makes it so interesting. So now as a prime example of this we [had] a president [Clinton] with high performance ratings and a vice president [Gore] who [was] well behind George W. Bush and Elizabeth Dole in early polls on the...presidential race....Well, I'm coming to believe (as I fight my way through this complexity) that while much of the public still [supported] Mr. Clinton, much of that same public [was] really very unhappy with the president's conduct and now [was] looking elsewhere for its next president. 'Elsewhere,' it appears, [meant] outside this scandal-scarred White House. And that judgment applies to Mr. Gore. (1999, 11)

Mental lock #7: The fear of making mistakes

Some students are motivated primarily to achieve; they're willing to take moderate risks and learn from their mistakes. They will usually avoid challenges that are either too easy or too hard. However, there are those who are more worried about making mistakes. Interestingly, these students tend to choose easy tasks where success is almost guaranteed or impossibly hard tasks that, ultimately, only serve to reinforce their fears of failure (McClelland, 1985).

Take the very confusing situation that existed with the conflict in the Balkans. What should the U.S. have done? What should NATO have done? When we intervened in Vietnam, we got ourselves into a terrible mess. When we sat on the sidelines in the 1930's, Hitler raged through

Europe and the cost in lives and destruction proved horrific. Did we exacerbate the loss of life when we began the bombing of Serbia because we feared repeating the mistakes of the past? Have we become too captive of particular historical "lessons?" Are those lessons still relevant today? Brown's (1999) history of the Balkan region can be helpful in confronting these issues.

> In the Balkans, armed conflict spread fast — from places unexpected, over soaring mountains, across ethnic divides, and into the conscience of Western leaders....It was the winter of 1997 when Albania imploded with the collapse of a group of pyramid bank schemes, sending thousands of scorned investors to the streets. The government fell, then the police, and soon rioters had seized some 100,000 weapons from military stocks.... Meanwhile in neighboring Serbia, the archenemy of Albania ...[demonstrations] over election fraud were reaching the danger level, and there was talk of revolution.... [Stolen guns] began seeping over the mountains, through the porous border on donkey carts, and into the southern Serbian province of Kosova [where]...ethnic Albanian guerrillas... were already preparing to fight for independence.
>
> With weapons, the war was on....Meanwhile, Macedonia, sandwiched in the middle and without a real army, looked on nervously, worried that its own restive ethnic Albanian population would be the next to call for independence. As Kosova exploded — villages razed, civilians massacred — the difficult questions it raised reached Bosnia, which was still recovering from a war of its own. Should the Muslims there support the Muslims in Kosova?...And what about Greece? Would it side with its Christian Orthodox cousins, the Serbs, and risk a greater conflict with its longtime enemy, Turkey, a fellow NATO member that would surely back the Muslim ethnic Albanians? More than any other region in Europe this century, the Balkans have been a constant source of instability. They are poor states, rife with nationalism and volatile ethnic mixes, the crossroads between East and West, Islam and Christianity, war and peace. (1999, 12-13)

Mental lock #8: The prohibitions against play and the commandment to be serious

Play can be a powerful force for creativity, spontaneity, energy, and very new thinking. For example, some of our computer breakthroughs have evolved from work on games. Fueled by fun, work becomes play. But there can be a deadly side to play. How ironic to think about "war games." Do computer and video killing games desensitize us to violence? Using the framework of Transactional Analysis, you can see both the upside and downside to the "Child" energy within each of us, the creative spontaneity or the angry rebelliousness we can express. In study groups, for example, students can get sidetracked and frustrated when someone in the group wants to play and the group gets off task. On the other hand, a group that can have fun together can balance some of the duller, repetitive work of study. With some understanding of group dynamics and some skill with communication, however, tensions can be part of a creative unfolding.

Mental lock #9: The assumption by many that they lack creativity

Opening these locks, insists von Oech, is something we all can and should do, and higher education can provide a wonderful opportunity to begin this process. Instructors and students alike really do have a license, even an obligation, to "whack" those old ways of thinking and consider new possibilities. The risks to our collective peace and prosperity are too great to do otherwise. We can all learn to embrace complexity and confront the big questions, to offer hypotheses and dream about possibilities, to take constructive and proactive steps towards a better future. Each of us can nurture a climate for ourselves that supports our own creative processes. We can take classes that stretch us in new and different ways — intellectually, emotionally, aesthetically, and physically. We can explore areas of art, music, theater, and philosophy. Every one of us has some element of creative potential within ourselves. How often has any of us heard the self-judgment, "I'm not creative at all." Just what will it take to move off this kind of self-defeating posture? For von Oech, it's mostly a matter of attitude, of breaking out of those mental locks. Peace on so many levels may depend on making that break.

Be cautious of the language trap

We might add one more potential trap to von Oech's list — call it the language or concept trap. Examining how we define peace is a good starting point for recognizing how our word choices can direct our creation of concepts concerning almost any subject.

Concepts of Peace

What does the word *peace* mean to you? What are the critical attributes? The absence of war? The absence of violence? Quiet? How quiet? The quiet before an attack can be terrifying. Most historians seem to agree that the punishing and humiliating peace that was imposed on Germany after World War I provided a fertile soil for Hitler and the Fascist drive for military power and vengeance. Who gets to define this word *peace*? For that matter, who decides when our dictionaries should be modified? Will students remember better a concept whose meaning they helped to *construct*? Will active participation in a cooperative project give them some concrete understanding of what it takes to "keep the peace" as a group works toward consensus?

In *Savage Dreams,* Rebecca Solnit (1994) describes the history of the Nevada Basin from the time when Europeans first entered the area in the early nineteenth century. The words you choose to describe these events can make a great deal of difference in how you think about them, whether you see the Europeans as invaders or explorers, for example, and who must bear the responsibility for the bloodshed that ensued. Solnit describes the European perspective this way: "The white explorers of the Great Basin always read it as a place of death and finality, as a terminal futurity, and though from aesthetic perspectives it might have been sublime, from the pragmatic outlook of invaders it was simply a hostile, useless place" (p. 48). You would have to ask: Would the native peoples who had made the Nevada Basin their home for centuries have used this kind of language — "place of death," "terminal futility," a "hostile, useless place"?

The impact of language and the choice of concepts get even more complicated when you read how Solnit describes the intent of the other players and forces in this story.

The Hudson's Bay Company sent in a group of British trappers...led by Peter Skene Ogden. The British and American
trappers were engaged in a territorial battle over the West. The
British, through what was to become famous as their 'scorched
earth' campaign, intended to prevent American expansion into
the Great basin — the Hudson's Bay Company was out to de-
stroy every beaver in the region and leave it useless, finished, for
its purposes. (1994, 48)

Is the concept "trapper," then, far too limiting for defining accu-
rately what happened here? By using descriptors like "murderous" and
"cruel" we might draw a very different picture of the actors in this conflict
over beavers, resources, and land. By attempting to remove the beaver from
the environment, could the Hudson's Bay Company be indicted for something barbarous? Because the beaver was so important to the survival of the
native populations, could this kind of policy and practice be termed "genocidal?" Ironically, if you look closely at the language commonly used by
most Europeans at the time to describe native peoples in the new world, you
find words like "savages" and "heathen." Again, we have to ask: Who gets
to define the concepts we see in our textbooks today?

But there's more, and this time the brutality is on the American side.
Solnit continues with her account:

When another party of Americans, Joseph Walker's, came
through in 1833, it found nothing to trap on the Humboldt and
named it the Barren River. The party continued west and en-
countered some Paiutes who repeatedly asked the trappers to
smoke pipes with them. Walker became suspicious that these
peace invitations were some kind of delaying tactic, so he and his
party shot as many as they could. It is described as the first indig-
enous-white conflict of any scale in the Great Basin, though it
was more like a massacre. (1994, 49)

Did the conceptual lenses that framed Walker's worldview determine his decisions? Did he see himself as a profiteer, a businessman com-
peting for scarce resources? Or perhaps a warrior, fighting for American
rights against the agents of British imperialists? Does the ease with which
he was able to slaughter native peoples seeking peace reflect a racist sense of
superiority? If that is so, then should the American government be respon-

sible for some form of reparations, as we have insisted from the Germans in the aftermath of World War II and their responsibility for the holocaust?

EGOCENTRIC THINKING

Another way to think about concepts in general is to examine the degree to which we are bound up by our own experiences and unable to stretch toward other perspectives or ideas. Jean Piaget and Jerome Bruner, for example, have contributed much to our understanding about the shifts in thinking that occur as we develop intellectually. Early in life, we are captives of our own senses and experiences, what we can see, feel, smell, etc. As we grow older, as our language develops, we begin to develop concepts which we then use to explain what we've experienced.

The term "violence," for example, can represent a range of experiences, extending from what you've seen or perhaps experienced first hand to what you've read about. When you were young, you might have associated violence with the school bully or some cartoon character on television mixed in with what you saw on the news or in the movies. As an adult, however, you have now heard so much more, about killings and beatings, about the terrorist attacks on the World Trade Center and the subsequent military reprisals, about war in the Balkans and ethnic cleansing, about historic tensions in the Middle East and Northern Ireland, about the Gulf War and Vietnam. Your concept of violence is now undoubtedly multifaceted and complex, layered with thoughts, images, sounds, and feelings.

ASSIMILATION AND ACCOMMODATION

In Piaget's (1952) theories of development, two notions have special relevance to this discussion about concepts. *Assimilation* describes the process by which we incorporate new information into the ways we already think. In other words, if we think of Europeans as "settlers" of the Americas, then what Walker did to the Paiutes was either an aberration or somehow justified (these Indians were trying to delay his group). *Accommodation*, on the other hand, explains the changes we make in our thinking when we are confronted with new information that doesn't fit our existing mindset *(schema)*. In this particular case, we might rethink our earlier ideas and accept that some numbers of Europeans — not all, but some

— were indeed "barbarians." William Perry's (1999) model of cognitive development gives us yet another way to think about this complexity — moving past simplistic, dichotomous, "right-wrong" characterizations toward acceptance of multiple and varied perspectives as we develop an increasing ability to handle complex and ambiguous material.

Rules, Examples, and Critical Attributes

Here's another way to think about language and concepts. When you think about your own thinking (i.e., metacognition), what rules do you find yourself obeying? For example, does your own fear of conflict rule out any acceptance of radically different viewpoints? Even if you disagree with someone else's conclusions, can you understand the rules that person used? According to Robert Gagne (1985), rules allow you to interrelate various concepts in ways that make sense to you.

At the lowest levels of organization, however, Gagne describes how we *discriminate* among different characteristics of a concept. For example, could you tell the difference between "justifiable homicide" and "slaughter" as you examine the events surrounding the killing of those Paiutes by members of the Walker party? With some clarification of the concept of "killing," can you then see how concepts can be interrelated through rules? For example, was this incident unusual given the rest of Walker's exploits? Or was there a pattern of ruthlessness here that you could use to describe his behaviors generally?

According to Gagne, these kinds of rules (concept-chains) can then be linked into *higher order rules*. You might ask, for example, how influential were other background forces (economic, cultural, historic) on Walker's actions? Was the competition for profits, the lure of wealth, driving Walker? How much can be explained as an outgrowth of long-standing colonial rivalry between Americans, British, and other foreign powers as they competed for the new world? Or how much was it a function of religious beliefs about superior belief systems, or racist convictions about superior peoples? Understanding more about these "rules" provides another framework for analyzing our thinking. Understanding more about our mental traps can free our creativity and help us refine and deepen our thinking about peace.

Chapter 3

Preparing Yourself –
Staying Balanced & Centered

In the midst of conflict or stress, when your fears rise and your spirits sag — when injustice demands a response and apathy abounds — how good are you at rallying for change? How do you keep your balance and stay centered, grounded, and clear about what's important? What skills do you have to navigate troubled waters when your own anger threatens to spill out? What are you able to teach or model for others? Jailed as a conscientious objector, Jim Forest (2000, 84) remembered what helped him stay centered and survive prison life.

> [I'm reminded] of a postcard message I received from (Thich) Nhat Hanh, (the Vietnamese Buddhist Nobel Peace Prize recipient) while I was in prison, something very brief: "Do you remember the tangerine we ate when we were together? You're being there is like that tangerine. Eat it and be one with it. Tomorrow it will be no more" It helped me immensely to find some encouragement in approaching prison in a non-confrontational way — to take the experience bite by bite.

Like Forest, who faced a whole new set of characters and challenges but found great comfort in a focus on the present, we can benefit much by learning how to stay balanced and centered from Hanh's (1991) *Peace is the Way*. In particular, Hanh provides some wonderful ideas for the mindfulness that is possible for any of us in every day life, how routine activities can be experienced within a larger concern for peace, nonviolence, and social justice.

In her own work with Philippinos caught up in the volatile mix of poverty, activism, repression, and violence, Dorothy Friesen (2000) found prayer as a valuable mechanism for staying centered and being clear about core values.

> How could we cope with it? How could we respond? We felt powerless in the face of this violence, fueled by the military, with economic and political support from our American government....Economics and a healthy prayer life are deeply interrelated. Praying means readiness to let go of our certainty and to move ahead from where we are now. It demands that we take to the road again and again, leaving our houses, and looking forward to a new land. Praying demands the readiness to live a life in which we have nothing to lose, so that we can always begin afresh. Whenever we willingly choose this poverty, we make ourselves vulnerable, but we also become free to see the world as it really is. (2000, 126-127)

In *Journey to Center,* Thomas Crum (1997, 17-18) draws on his training in the martial arts to offer other ideas for staying clear and aligned.

> Center is about accepting the pressures of life. Center is about inviting change, not mindlessly holding on to a position. It takes courage to change our perspectives. It takes courage to examine which beliefs really work for us. It takes guts to get off a limiting, but often comfortable view and shift to a larger point of view. When we're lost in a densely wooded area, it helps our perspective to move to higher ground. This enables us to witness our position — not in isolation but in relation to everything around us. We can all learn, each moment, to pierce through our cluttered thoughts to a higher purpose, and journey to higher ground. It is a path of learning and magic. It is the center of the storm.

Athletes talk about this awareness, this ability to focus in the moment, to quiet their nerves and the commotion all around. Likewise, actors must concentrate to respond to their cues, move through their lines, and create believable characters. Lawyers prepare their cases in advance but then must be able to respond to whatever emerges in the courtroom. In a very similar way, teachers must organize their course material and be prepared to respond to what students need and the environment demands.

Crum identifies three principles for staying centered. The first is to *acknowledge.* Identify the issues and players. What's at stake? Who is involved? Who needs to be involved? Second, Crum recommends *acceptance,* an awareness that there are reasons why people believe and act the way that they do. Understanding these reasons, then, becomes a foundation for moving beyond blame toward some resolution. Here the skills of *deep listening* and *empathy* become important, what Carl Rogers championed in his pioneering work on a client-centered, humanistic approach to counseling. These skills become that much more important when people explore their differences and attempt to move past their disagreements.

Accordingly, to approach peace constructively, we want a process of *respectful engagement*, leaving the exact nature of the way forward to the creative intelligence of the participants. In his autobiography, Nelson Mandela (1994) describes the importance of his concern for the Afrikaner guards on Robben Island during his twenty-seven year imprisonment, how his own understanding of their obligation allowed him to avoid the danger of becoming captive of his own anger.

> Even in the grimmest times in prison, when my comrades and I were pushed to our limits, I would see a glimmer of humanity in one of our guards, perhaps just for a second, but it was enough to reassure me and keep me going. Man's goodness is a flame that can be hidden but never extinguished. (p. 622)

Crum's third principle for centering is to *adapt,* to be willing to change and open up to new ideas. The creative process demands that we be able to rethink our ideas, what we have always done and where we could go. Our skills as instructors are tested from our very first teaching assignment. Advances in technology push us to explore new possibilities. The ability to adapt allows us to traverse that great divide between our own preparation, what we do in front of a class, and what our students need. The ability to adapt lets us respond to the unique dynamics of every class, the questions we get, the personalities, background, and motivation of our students.

On a physical level, Crum makes frequent reference to the power of meditation, to correct breathing, as one way to slow down and retain a clear focus. Another is positive visualization, to stop and "see" yourself teaching as you would like to — energized, insightful, resourceful, even inspiring. These practices can be helpful when you think about the groups you lead and the directions you want to go. Incorporated as part of daily practice, finding the space and quiet to reflect, can help you whenever tensions rise and conflicts emerge.

For Gandhi, finding centering — in the midst of turmoil, threat, sacrifice, and the pressures of living his life on such a large and conflicted stage — was always about clarity of purpose and self-discipline. Centering was an extension of his faith into his daily practice of meditation, and that link meant everything. Jesuit priest, peace activist, and scholar, John Dear (2000) described this interrelationship this way:

> [Nonviolence] was never simply a tactic. For Gandhi, it "is a matter of the heart." From his inner unity, through years of discipline and renunciation, Gandhi found the ability to suffer for justice's sake, to refuse to harm others, to go to prison for peace. For his friends in the independence movement, he wrote an essay, "How to Enjoy Jail." Such an essay came as the fruit of inner freedom already realized. Gandhi's nonviolence starts from within and moves outward. (2000, 113)

Once you have started this centering within and gotten a taste of how peace feels, you can move outward to deal with the larger climate of the classroom.

Chapter 4

PREPARING THE CLASSROOM CLIMATE

Classroom morale, teaching, and learning are inextricably linked in a very dynamic relationship. These interactions are well documented by a rich literature from business and organizational psychology that describes the many and varied ways in which employee morale directly impacts productivity. The loyalty that companies and institutions show to their workers tends to pay substantial returns by fostering a security that allows for more creative initiative and risk taking. Similar forces are at play in the classroom (Timpson and Bendel-Simso, 1996). Students value the enthusiasm that their professors bring to class and to their subjects. In turn, we love it when students show initiative. Nothing will kill a class more quickly than unwilling participants. As we ask students, ourselves, and each other to do more to promote peace and nonviolence, we can help by nurturing a positive classroom climate.

Nothing occurs in a vacuum. To support their learning, students draw much from a sense of safety and trust, from the presence of mutual respect and open communication. By and large, research suggests that student satisfaction with the quality of college teaching offers a foundation for challenging students to think more outside the competitive, win-lose, and hierarchical models that dominate economic and political thinking, in particular. For example, in one of the largest and best constructed surveys of academic climate on campus, Arthur Levine and Jeanette Cureton (1998) paint a rather rosy picture:

> The vast majority [of students] attest to being satisfied with their college overall and would rather be going to college now than doing anything else....As for the quality of teaching at their institutions, students are even more pleased. Despite a sea of complaints in the press about the quality of college teaching, students interviewed on our site visits singled out faculty over and over again as being caring and anxious to help. (1998, 130)

Recall the classes you enjoyed most as a student, where you learned the most. Ask yourself why. What factors affected your motivation and your learning? How were these linked? Learning is always a "co-constructed" endeavor. Teaching and learning are shared responsibilities. Instructors need to bring expertise, preparation, enthusiasm, creativity, and a variety of skills to facilitate learning. Students need to bring a motivation to learn, their intelligence, and creativity, their own experiences, a willingness to help, and support others as well as some understanding about what is required for learning in a group context. A positive climate for learning is then co-created. The best conceived and most creatively delivered presentation or activity will fall flat if students don't care. In turn, the most motivated students may wilt in the face of an excessively dry delivery and uncaring instructors. As instructors, we can insist on the kinds of processes that support an exploration of peaceful alternatives to conflict.

The Characteristics
of a Positive Classroom Climate

A positive climate allows us as instructors, whatever our disciplines, to challenge students and maximize learning without fear of emotional meltdowns or unnecessary resistance to change. Research into the underpinnings of classroom climate reach back many years. In the seventies, CFK Limited, a Denver-based philanthropic foundation dedicated to improving the learning environment of schools, supported the publication of a series of monographs detailing what "educational climate" meant and how schools can use these ideas to improve. In one of these publications, Shaheen and Pedrick (1974) defined *climate* in terms of productivity (learning, thinking) and satisfaction (morale).

For these researchers, *productivity* went beyond the acquisition of basic knowledge to include factors we would also associate with critical and creative thinking:

- Achieving basic skills.

- Developing constructive attitudes.

- Developing and expanding an adequate knowledge base.

- Clarifying values and purposes.

- Utilizing inquiry and problem-solving processes.

Satisfaction, they then argued, was inextricably linked to productivity and could be assessed through the following:

- Gaining a sense of personal worth.

- Enjoying school as a pleasant place to live and work.

- Gaining rewards from participation in worthwhile activities.

At about the same time, Fox and his group (1974) outlined several general factors that characterize a positive educational climate generally, including respect, trust, high morale, opportunities for input, continuous professional growth, cohesiveness, renewal, caring, commitment to goals, and ease of communication. In 1980, Lezotte and his colleagues focused on productivity as it relates to measurable learning outcomes, i.e., the norms, beliefs, and attitudes that enhance or impede student achievement.

If you need more evidence of this interrelationship, consider the work of Joseph Lowman (1995) who makes reference to climate when he focuses on those factors that drive learning in college. For Lowman, it all boils down to two elements: *Intellectual excitement* and *rapport*. In his view, the best instructors in college combine enthusiasm for their course material with a genuine care for students and their learning. These kinds of respectful processes are especially important when addressing differences and resolving conflicts at any level — local, national, or international.

Trust and Achievement

However, whenever you do push for deeper, more thoughtful responses from students, you have probably heard the popular plea, "Just tell us what we need to know for the test." Physicist Sandy Kern has always resisted a focus on memorized, acquired knowledge that lacks any transferable understanding. Foregoing what is easier, more conventional, and more comfortable for students, he pushes and probes for something deeper. Admittedly the outcomes may be illusive to gauge, for we can never really get into the heads of students to know precisely how they're thinking. Each of us makes educated guesses based on student performance on exams, assignments, projects, and the like, especially when we're trying to assess higher levels of reasoning. Professors like Kern also make inferences from student responses in class.

Sitting in his class, you can see Kern watching closely for signs of confusion even when he is lecturing. He'll often poll a class to test student thinking or perform a simple demonstration, for example, throwing a ball in the air and then asking about the forces at work on the ball after it leaves the hand. (He's an avid baseball fan!) "Is it the force of the throw or gravity at play here?" Because many students are understandably anxious, some even terrified, about admitting their confusions in a class of three hundred, Kern will go to some lengths to make the climate safer for student participation. A poll is one way since everyone is asked to make a response. But he has also stopped after working on a problem and said to his class, "Look, there is no such thing as a foolish question, only a foolish answer, so I'm the only one at risk here."

"Safety" for students to participate actively in class involves a variety of forces. Abraham Maslow (1959) has constructed one of the most widely referenced theories about the factors that underlie learning and growth. His hierarchy of needs looks like the following:

1: Physiological needs   **Deficiency**

2: Safety needs   **Deficiency**

3: Love and belonging needs   **Deficiency**

4: Self-esteem needs   **Deficiency**

5: Need for self-actualization   **Growth**

At the first level and before students can get on with anything else, they have certain *physiological needs* like food, liquid, sleep. These are not trivial issues for those who juggle work, limited financial resources, and play, with heavy academic loads.

At the next level up, students require a sense of physical and psychological *safety* if they are to participate fully. Do they feel that they can speak up in their classes without being put down, that their ideas will be respected by their instructor and classmates. Of course, this may all be about their "perception" of safety and may reflect personal insecurities and anxieties. One way forward is to help students see that, in fact, no real threat may exist. Will others really be critical if they speak up or make a mistake? And whose problem is it if someone disagrees or challenges what they say? In truth, everyone benefits when we can air differences of opinion in an open and respectful context.

At the third level, a sense of *love* and *belonging* adds some measure of community, group support and friendship. It can be difficult for students to focus and persevere when they feel isolated. Helping them to get to know some of their classmates can make a big difference in their willingness to take risks. When they are thrown into large classes in that first semester on campus, they often feel intimidated, especially if they're far from home and friends and have been accustomed to small high school classes. Forming study groups, for example, has helped many students create small, supportive communities within large classes. The peace movement, of course, has always drawn on the collective action of demonstrations, protests, petition drives, and the like to build a sense of loyalty and community.

Maslow's fourth level addresses *self-esteem* — how good any of us feels about ourselves and the confidence we have in our own abilities. Experiencing some success often engenders optimism. Repeated failure can take a toll on our psyche. A course built on the principles of mastery, for example, of achieving success as a prerequisite for moving on, can help nurture the independent thinkers we all want to create and be.

While the first four levels reflect areas of need, the fifth and final level is one of growth, what Maslow referred to as *self-actualization,* where we can seek out new ideas, information, skills or experiences. Here is where we are able to take reasonable risks, knowing we have the self-confidence to learn from our mistakes. Large and small measures can contribute to a classroom climate that is especially important for addressing conflicts and finding constructive solutions.

For example, James Treat is a Native American professor who puts his classes in a circle whenever he can. He wants the connectedness this kind of room arrangement provides. Discussions are better, livelier when students can see each other. However, it's more than that for Treat because the circle represents an important cultural tradition, one that respects everyone's contributions. Straight rows facing the front put the responsibility on one person to lead. The community becomes hierarchical. The physical design of our classes and how we organize instruction can help connect us with our students and them with each other. This is one of the many ways that attention to the classroom environment builds a foundation that is crucially important for maximizing learning and promoting peacemaking.

Chapter 5

ESTABLISHING
COMMUNICATION

We all know that good classroom communication can be pivotal in defusing a volatile confrontation, helping everyone lower their emotions and defenses in order to get a deeper understanding of what happened, how people feel about it, and what peaceful alternatives are possible. This chapter draws on Tom Gordon's (1974) *Teacher Effectiveness Training* to describe three sets of skills that provide an effective model for establishing good communication: deep listening, empathetic expressing, and consensus.

DEEP LISTENING

There are many different forms of listening. There is the "light" listening you do in passing with friends or colleagues, or in response to *"What's up?"* or *"How about those Rams!"* (Insert your team's name or mascot.) You'll usually engage in more "professional" listening in class when questions arise or a discussion unfolds. You might experience some "anxious" listening when you sit down for your annual performance review.

Then there is the "ceremonial" listening amidst the pomp of a graduation exercise, or the "haphazard" listening when you're watching TV. Then there is "deep" listening, the kind you do when a friend has a problem and needs your support and assistance, when a loved one has died, the kind of listening you need when a rejection letter arrives.

Some guidelines for this deeper form of listening can help you and your students when you are trying to resolve a problem. It's helpful to know that this option is available when needed. The benefits can last a lifetime. Steven Covey's (1989) *The Seven Habits of Highly Effective People* describes some of these skills within a context of business. Tom Gordon's (1974) *Teacher Effectiveness Training* describes the benefits of deep listening in classrooms.

Seek first to understand

Too often, our own agendas and our need to be heard make it difficult to listen deeply to someone else, to give our undivided attention. Disciplining yourself to put your own needs on hold and attend to someone else can help that person — and you — get to a better understanding about a particular problem, to see more clearly from that person's perspective.

In a small group section of a first year seminar dedicated to helping students make a successful transition from high school to college, we took quite a bit of time to discuss the experience of one of the students — let's call her Andrea — and her experience proved to be a wonderful case study that had meaning for everyone in the class.

Andrea was really frustrated by the duplication she saw in her chemistry class, between what was in the text and what was covered in lecture. "I can read," she told us. "I don't need to be read to, word for word." Moreover, her entire chemistry class seemed to be in revolt, with far too many students coming in late, leaving early, talking during lecture, reading the newspaper, etc. Chaos ruled and it was ugly. In Andrea's mind, students were being really rude, very disrespectful! When she went to her instructor to complain, she first tried to understand why all this was happening.

What she learned was that the instructor, just out of her own graduate program, was anxious about doing well and eager to follow the advice of a senior faculty mentor who told her to stay "close to the text." Once Andrea heard that, she understood. Instead of writing her off as incompetent, uncaring, or just plain dull, Andrea could see that the instructor was trapped by poor advice and a desire to do well. What Andrea needed in class were examples that would illustrate the text, that would provide concrete and accessible references for various chemical theories and concepts. After hearing Andrea's concerns and recommendations, the instructor thanked her for coming in to talk (and listen), promised that she would rethink her future lectures and hoped that Andrea would come back with more feedback in the future.

HELP CLARIFY THOUGHTS AND FEELINGS

Once you understand a situation better, you then want to focus on the other person's thoughts and feelings. You become a kind of *sounding board*, reflecting back what you hear and what you sense, how the other might feel. Typically, the other person will either confirm that you got it right or correct you. Either way, each of you is sharpening your understanding of the issues and underlying causes.

By mirroring back in this manner, you are also conveying your desire to understand. Intentions matter! One of the greatest gifts you can give anyone is your support, assistance, and undivided attention. You do care what that person thinks and feels. With this kind of interactive focus, you're building trust, as you move toward a deeper understanding. The barriers drop away. Many of us regularly think out loud. Having someone listen carefully, in the way I am describing here, can help any of us clarify our own thoughts and feelings, move past our frustrations, and toward some constructive resolution.

On the emotional side, be alert to nonverbal messages and your own intuition about how the other person is feeling, how volatile or charged a particular problem is for that person. Check out your hunches. Andrea might have offered to her instructor, "You seem really trapped between what you were told and what we are saying that we need." Or "If I were in your situation, I would be really frustrated." The chemistry instructor could have confirmed or corrected Andrea's guesses and their mutual trust might have deepened.

Minimize questioning

The problem with questioning is that it comes from you, the listener, and can take the ownership of the process away from the other person. Your questions might help you clarify something, but they may also distract the other person from going deeper, from following his or her self-reflections and insights. The primary goal should always be to help the other person clarify his or her thoughts and feelings. This is a subtle but useful distinction. It's not an iron-clad principle but a dynamic that we can be alert to as instructors.

For example, you can use reflective statements instead of questions: "You seem really upset about this." This may seem like a small point, but when you put it in question form — "Are you upset about this?" — you've taken over the direction of the conversation. You're demanding a response. In contrast, reflections keep the responsibility on the other person to control the process, to clarify, and decide how to move on. You want to be a supportive sounding board, not an interrogator.

Keep your own opinions on hold

Finally, be cautious about "hitchhiking," jumping into the conversation with your own experiences, opinions, etc. In casual conversations there is this natural dynamic of back and forth, give and take, often rapid and overlapping. But when you want to listen deeply or help someone embroiled in a conflict, disciplining yourself to keep the focus on the other may be the best approach. In the model we are describing here, you begin with two assumptions: first, that the other person knows best the particulars of his or her situation; and second, that it's best to let that other person decide when to ask for advice or to hear about your experiences. Offering too much too soon can undermine that person's self-confidence and ability to see through a problem.

In the short run, your advice might be very helpful, but it is still your advice. In the long run, you may be a better friend or instructor by holding back your own ideas until a time when the other person has wrestled with all the issues and now is asking for your help. In the daily scheme of things, few of us function like this, so it may take some real self-discipline and feedback to get there. And time! Give it a try when you get the chance.

THE CLEARNESS COMMITTEE

Another way to approach this process of deep listening comes from Parker Palmer (1998), a former college instructor who writes and consults about teaching, learning, philosophy, and spirituality, how to get more than information across, how to address deeper needs of the heart and soul. What he describes here may seem strange, perhaps because it is so different from the ways most of us tend to communicate on a daily basis. Yet, this process bears study; in part, because it has evolved from a faith-based tradition that has always been committed to nonviolence and peace as an article of faith.

> I have had some experience with a model for this way of being together. It comes from a branch of the Quaker community that for more than three centuries has done without the benefit of clerical leadership. In order to do work that most churches do via ordained leaders — like helping people with the issues in their lives — these Quakers had to invent social structures that would allow members to do such work with and for each other. (1998, 151)

Here's how the clearness committee model can work. When a member is struggling and seeking help, four or five others are invited in to support. First, however, the member or "focus person" must do some writing or journaling about the problem. The writing should include a clear statement about the issue or conflict, the essence of the struggle; then, something about its importance in the context of that person's life, experiences and background; and finally, some thoughts about the future, how this problem threatens to play out and what that means to him or her.

The group then meets for two to three hours, sitting in a circle and giving its undivided attention to the person in need. No "rushing in to give comfort." No sharing of experiences that might be distracting. For clearness committee members this means acting as if *they* "had no other purpose on earth than to care for this human being." Committee members are "forbidden to speak to the focus person in any way except to ask that person an honest, open question." Time slows down during this kind of meeting. It's not a "cross-examination." The focus person can pass on a particular question. Everyone allows enough time and silence to elapse so that the process is "respectful and gentle."

The ground rules are simple for committee members. They keep their own advice on hold. They do not "over-identify" and take responsibility away from the focus person; e.g., "Oh, that happened to me and I ...." They refrain from offering suggestions, books or activities for example. Instead, they ask honest, open questions which can help the focus person "discover wisdom within." As Palmer (1994, 154) reminds us:

> As the process unfolds, we are reminded of a simple truth: because we cannot get inside another person's soul, we cannot possibly know the answer to another person's problem. Indeed, we cannot even know what exactly the problem is. I am often reminded of this fact when I serve as a member of a clearness committee. Ten minutes into the proceedings, I feel certain that I know what is wrong with the focus person and how to fix it. But after two hours of attentive listening, I am appalled at my earlier arrogance. I see now that I did not understand — and even if I did, my abstract concept of the problem is meaningless until understanding arises within the person whose problem it is.

EMPATHIC EXPRESSING

Empathic expressing is the second set of skills that Gordon identifies in *Teacher Effectiveness Training*. These skills also played a part in the case of Andrea and her chemistry instructor. From Andrea's perspective, the chemistry class bordered on a waste of time; her frustration was rising. I encouraged Andrea and others to approach their instructor with some forethought, (1) to understand the problem from the instructor's point of view, (2) to offer a clear analysis based on their own experiences, and then (3) to make a clear and responsible request. This model of "empathic expressing" offers some structure for discussing difficult issues or conflicts with someone else. It builds on mutual understanding, empathy, and trust as a foundation for effective communication.

When her chemistry class met again, Andrea walked up after class and repeated what she had practiced in our small group discussion section, "Hi. You know, a lot of us are struggling in this class and some examples would really help. I like it when you explain what's in the book. I read the material outside of class but I need help with understanding it." The teacher smiled and said, "Sure. I can try to do that." In subsequent classes, Andrea reported that she could see some improvements. So she went up again and told this teacher how she appreciated the effort, that it was making a difference. What a mood shift for Andrea. From being just another whiner, she took some initiative, identified her needs and frustrations, expressed some empathy, and offered a solution. Her whole attitude about this class changed as well. Not that everything turned around immediately, but she did move off the negative and toward a positive, constructive, and assertive approach to the problem she was having. Empathy helped her make this shift and build a better communication bridge with her instructor.

DESCRIPTION OF THE PROBLEM

Empathic expressing begins with a clear description of the problem. Andrea was bored with a mere repetition of what was in the text. She usually was up-to-date for class with her readings. She needed explanations, concrete examples to make sense of the theories, concepts, and principles but didn't know how she could get the help she needed in such a large lecture class. Although it took some time in our own class, with the collective help of her classmates we did finally get through her frustrations and identify the problem affecting her learning.

I-MESSAGE

The next step was to practice with language that would keep the ownership of the issue with Andrea and her experience. Instead of leading with criticism — "You know, the way you teach is boring" — we shifted to a statement of feelings: "When you just review what is in the book, I get really frustrated…." or "…I feel bored." No one can argue with Andrea's experience and feelings here. It's not as if there is some objective point beyond which a class automatically becomes boring for every student. An I-message is more honest and personal; you have to own your own feelings, but you also understand that no one can take those feelings away or judge them as "wrong."

A REASON WHY

The next step is to give a reason for your feelings, an explanation. The immature child will pout, "I'm bored" but have no explanation of why or idea about a solution. "Fix it, mom" or "Entertain me, dad" is the underlying message. For Andrea, giving a reason meant saying, "When you just lecture from the text, I do get bored and frustrated because I read the material already. However, I do have questions and I need some help."

Express empathy

The next step for Andrea was to *show* some empathy for what her instructor might be feeling. We discussed a number of possibilities. Because this was a young teacher, we thought about using the following response: "I know you must be nervous and want to stay close to the assigned readings. I know this is your very first teaching assignment." The instructor was right out of graduate school and wanted to do well as a stepping stone to a permanent position somewhere else. She was commuting sixty plus miles each way and was largely cut off from other faculty. Moreover, she had been advised by the course coordinator to "stay close to the text." Andrea's attempt at empathy was right on target — the instructor *was* anxious — and, in return, Andrea got a better understanding about why. This instructor was a real person with real feelings.

Identify a positive

Important in communication about a problem is to hold out the expectation that a solution is possible. In this case Andrea said the following: "I know the lectures can work better for me. When you gave examples or stopped to answer questions, it made a real difference. It helped me get the idea better." Here, Andrea was providing a concrete example (herself) of something that helped.

Make a clear request

Instead of simply asking this instructor to "do better," instead of just leaving it up to her to figure out a solution, Andrea offered the following. "I would like you to add more examples in your lectures. These help a lot. I'd also like you to stop and ask for questions more often. And I'll try to see you after class or during office hours if there is something I am still confused about." Although it took some time to work through these steps and although the very idea of approaching an instructor in a big lecture class to say all this seemed frightening at first, taking this kind of initiative made a big difference for Andrea. She learned some important lessons about advocating for herself in a responsible and effective manner.

CONSENSUS

Consensus is the third set of skills that Gordon identifies as critical in *Teacher Effectiveness Training.* An example from the world of peacemaking may help. In *Savage Dreams,* Rebecca Solnit (1994) traces the interconnections between the history of nuclear weapons testing and the environmental movement. She and her brother were both activists and she describes her experiences with consensus this way.

> [My] little brother is an anarchist, and a key organizer for the antinuclear movement, and though he was initially an anarchist in the sense that innumerable punks were in the eighties, he has read his Bakunin and Kropotkin and is now very seriously an anarchist. Anarchy, I should explain, means not the lack of order but of hierarchy, a direct and absolute democracy. Voting democracy, as anarchists point out, simply allows a majority to impose its will on a minority and is not necessarily participatory or direct. They themselves continue the process of negotiation until all participants achieve consensus, until everyone — not merely a majority — has arrived at a viable decision. Anarchy proper usually works out to mean excruciatingly interminable meetings, rather than the mayhem the word evokes in most American imaginations....I have never found the patience and tolerance necessary to work with group consensus for extended periods. (1994, 12-14)

Finding consensus within any group can have significant payoffs although there are associated costs of time and effort. Whether you yourself are working on a big collaborative project or participating on a committee, whether your students are trying to get a study group organized or just finding common ground with a roommate, having some guidelines for navigating this kind of interpersonal terrain can help. When everyone can agree, you can get more commitment for the decisions you make. You can also get better decisions when everyone's voice is heard and a variety of perspectives surface. You can even get more creative decisions. Admittedly, diverse viewpoints, experiences and personalities can make for a degree of tension in any process, especially if everyone is in a hurry. Consensus invariably takes more time, but there are important benefits. Here is a listing of recommended guidelines you could use in any number of situations.

Define the problem

If students are meeting to form a study group, for instance, it can be useful if they begin by focusing on course requirements and what they'll need to do — when and where to meet and for how long, what to bring and how responsibilities might be best shared. Looking over past exams can give them some additional clues.

Brainstorm

It's important to understand the benefits of brainstorming, particularly that by reserving judgment at this point in the process you can get a lot of different ideas out for discussion. Sometimes the better and more creative ideas only surface after students have worked through the more obvious ones. The key here is to generate ideas, as many as possible, without stopping to evaluate. No matter how strange these ideas may sound, students can help promote consensus by getting them all out and on their list before they start to eliminate any.

For example, Chuck was another student in our first year seminar. He organized a study group for his toughest class, chemistry. Together, members of the group looked over sample test questions and realized that they really did understand the material. Instead of reserving some time each week to review their notes, they decided to meet the day before the exam for a couple of hours. In that way they would be psyched, focused, and efficient. And it worked, at least for the first exam. Taking the time to think through their needs and honestly assess their motivations produced a plan that worked. They were also able to avoid some needless meetings and wasted time. There are times when peacemaking can be proactive, when conflicts are avoided through effective planning and organization.

Identify consequences

This stage helps you go a bit further and think about the implications of your various choices. For Chuck and his group there was a bit of a gamble as to whether the night before would be enough. However, they did believe that scheduling study time earlier would only generate frustrations and undermine their motivation. When you aim for consensus, you take a little more time to think things through instead of impulsively latching on to whatever everyone else is doing or whatever the conventional wisdom is.

Decide

At this stage groups need to make a decision. One guideline many find useful is to keep any agreements tentative, like a trial run. In that way, students can assess their success early on without being so locked in that change becomes impossible. To get some movement toward consensus, they can think of a decision as an experiment. People can often agree to that.

Reevaluate and modify if necessary

When Chuck and his study group got their results from the second exam — and they didn't do as well compared to the first exam — they re-thought their plans and decided that they would need to meet earlier and more frequently for the third exam, that perhaps they had gotten a bit lucky on the first exam or had been over-confident and then slacked off too much in their note-taking and engagement in class. At any rate, they channeled their disappointment with their second exam results into a revised plan for their study time together.

Additional thoughts on group consensus

It can also be helpful if everyone in a group understands and agrees to these guidelines. In this way, they can get real ownership in the process and their group's decision. Having group members take on various roles can also help. Someone could be the recorder, for example, another the task master, another the time keeper, another the synthesizer or summarizer. The moderator's role is the peacemaker for a group, attentive to feelings and alert to resolving any conflicts that arise. On the other hand, groups can also have everyone conscious of each of these roles and let the responsibilities for their functioning be more fluid. The explorations in Chapter 8 will further explain the ways in which the skills of cooperation can help with various group projects and activities.

There can be no doubt that deep listening, empathetic expressing, and consensus-making provide a useful model for establishing good communications in the classroom. They also establish the kind of communication skills that underlie effective efforts in peacemaking. To keep those skills in good working order, we also have to be able to understand and manage our emotions.

Chapter 6

Understanding
& Managing Emotions

My colleague and long-time friend, Eric Larsen, teaches in an alternative high school where young people get a second chance. Too often caught up in a deadly cycle of drugs and alcohol, rebelling and fighting, they are ripe for learning about the choices they have and alternatives to what they're currently doing. One effective way that Eric uses to help them learn is to build up their "skills," their ideas for how to manage the feelings that often got them into trouble. Eric attends to the emotional intelligence necessary for peaceful, nonviolent, and constructive alternatives through his Discovery Program.

Students and instructors alike can benefit from knowing more about how their "emotional intelligence" and how assertiveness training and Transactional Analysis, for example, can help them build skills to deal with complex and difficult situations where strong feelings may surface. The essential skills for peacemaking can be taught if the motivation is there to do so.

With his roots in the Quaker tradition, Parker Palmer (1998) offers ideas for managing both emotions and the intellect, ideas that can also support peacemaking. In his very popular *The Courage to Teach,* he addresses the complexities of teaching and the importance of more holistic approaches that integrate head and heart, the "both-and" mixture of what he terms "paradoxical teaching."

> Intellect works in concert with feeling, so if I hope to open my students' minds, I must open their emotions as well. None of these truths about teaching can be approached as a simple either-or, though in academic culture we constantly try to do so...What I want is a richer, more paradoxical model of teaching and learning than binary thought allows, a model that reveals how the paradox of thinking and feeling are joined — whether we are comfortable with paradox or not....When a person is healthy, the head and the heart are both-and, not either-or, and teaching that honors that paradox can help make us more whole. (1998, 63-64)

EMOTIONAL INTELLIGENCE

In a series of books that have become especially popular with K-12 teachers, Howard Gardner (1983, 1999a, 199b) identifies six "intelligences" beyond the traditional foci on mathematical reasoning and reading comprehension. Two of these are about emotions: the *intrapersonal* intelligence that governs our abilities to reflect and be self aware; and the *interpersonal* intelligence that determines our abilities to work cooperatively with others.

Daniel Goleman (1994) attracted wide attention from the general public in a book that focuses on these same emotional skills which, he insists, have much more to do with success in life than raw brain power. It's a compelling argument since we all know bright people who are miserable as team members, or creative types who seem isolated, depressed, and too often self-destructive. In addition, we all know lots of seemingly average folks who have the energy, the charm, even the charisma needed to rally others and get amazing things done.

In the opening pages of *Earth in Mind,* David Orr (1994) rips into conventional wisdom about intelligence when environmental destruction and violence are committed by some of the brightest and best educated.

If today is a typical day on planet earth, we will lose another 72 square miles of rain forest, or about an acre a second...We will lose 40 to 250 species....And today we will add 2,700 tons of chlorofluorocarbons and 15 million tons of carbon dioxide to the atmosphere...The truth is that many things on which our future health and prosperity depend are in dire jeopardy....It is worth noting that this is not the work of ignorant people. Rather, it is largely the result of work by people with BAS, BSs, LLBs, MBAs, and PhDs. Elie Wiesel once made the same point, noting that the designers and perpetrators of Auschwitz, Dachau, and Buchenwald — the Holocaust — were the heirs of Kant and Goethe, widely thought to be the best educated people on earth. (1994, 7)

In a later chapter, Orr goes on to write that

real intelligence depends upon character as much as it does on mental horsepower....[Whole] civilizations can be simulta- neously clever and stupid....As Exhibit A, consider our phe- nomenal and growing computer capabilities side by side with our decaying inner cities, insensate violence, various addic- tions, rising public debt, and the destruction of nature all around us. Can it be that we are in fact becoming more clever and less intelligent? (1994, 51)

In a parallel vein, Goleman (1994) critiques conventional views of in- telligence as much too narrow given what is required for success in life: ef- fective management of our emotions and reactions, our anger and compassion, our abilities to form relationships and navigate effectively within and between groups.

There are widespread exceptions to the rule that IQ predicts success — many (or more) exceptions than cases that fit the rule. At best, IQ contributes about 20 percent to the factors that determine life success, which leaves 80 percent to other forces....My concern is with a key set of these 'other character- istics,' emotional intelligence: abilities such as being able to motivate oneself and persist in the face of frustrations; to con- trol impulse and delay gratification; to regulate one's moods and keep distress from swamping the ability to think; to empathize and to hope. (1994, 34)

At the end of his book, Goleman has a section he titles, "The ABC's of Emotional Intelligence." Think about your own experiences with conflicts, personal and professional, your feelings about nonviolent alternatives generally. What would happen if you took the time to educate your students about these options? It's hard to argue with Goleman's contention that understanding and managing our emotional responses are foundational for success. As an instructor, you can help students in a number of ways:

- Develop self-awareness, in the sense of recognizing feelings and building a vocabulary for them, and seeing the links between thoughts, feelings, and reactions;

- Know if thoughts or feelings are ruling a decision;

- See the consequences of alternative choices;

- Apply these insights to decisions about such issues as fighting, drugs, alcohol, smoking, and sex;

- Recognize strengths and weaknesses, and seeing self in a positive but realistic light;

- Realize what is behind a feeling (for example, the hurt that triggers anger);

- Learn ways to handle anxieties, anger, and sadness;

- Take responsibility for decisions and actions, and follow through on commitments;

- Empathize — understanding others' feelings and taking their perspective;

- Respect differences in how people feel about things;

- Learn to be a good listener and question-asker;

- Distinguish between what someone says or does and their own reactions and judgments;

- Become assertive rather than angry or passive;

- Learn the arts of cooperation, conflict resolution, and negotiating compromise.

ASSERTIVENESS

Many of the skills of peacemaking have emerged from work with at-risk populations. Assertiveness training helps students distinguish between aggressive, assertive, and submissive responses. Invariably, it is when people let their emotions fuel their aggressive tendencies that violence erupts. Unfortunately, it can also be true that retreating to a submissive state can feed a bully's aggressive tendencies. I don't want to "blame the victim" or excuse the bully but rather suggest that there can be a very unhealthy co-dependent cycle of violence that develops and needs to be confronted in all who are involved.

It is that place in between aggressive and submissive responses where the assertive response lies, delivered with confidence, usually face to face, and with direct eye contact. As such it offers the clearest and most effective communication. While college classrooms rarely see outbreaks of violence, frustrations are quite common when students feel lost or confused, dismissed, challenged, picked on, or ignored. For example, group projects often leave some students feeling exploited as workloads play out unfairly amid different learning and communication styles.

Assertiveness training has proven enormously useful for many adults as well as the young. The Canters' *Assertive Discipline* has been popular among teachers since its publication in 1976. Students can also benefit from understanding more about the continuum of choices they have, what distinguishes an assertive response from aggressive or submissive responses.

At one end of this continuum, we can get hostile. We can get angry, adopt a negative attitude, or become aggressive. We could blame someone else — a colleague, the students or their parents, the culture. Students often blame the content or the text (labeling it boring), and are unwilling to dig much for any deeper meanings. Students may also act out in class in a variety of ways, being rude to instructors and classmates alike, coming in late or leaving early, chatting with friends. Even doodling and sleeping, eating, or reading the newspaper can be passive-aggressive expressions of disrespect or rebellion.

On the other end of this continuum, we can play a submissive role and allow others to dominate or some injustice to continue. At times it may just be inertia that wins. Or we let our confusions paralyze us. We may suffer in silence or look for excuses. We may define ourselves as introverts and be uncomfortable out front. We may feel overwhelmed by events that seem too big, too dangerous, or too far away. Students will often succumb to peer pressure and limit their participation in class, pulling those ball caps lower over their eyes or around backwards, slumping down, and checking out. In their minds, being "cool" may undermine their learning. In a study group, a submissive role may mean backing off from taking initiative. It can be hard for students to confront each other about lousy attitudes, lack of responsibility, off-task behavior, or the like.

Taking some time to discuss and practice assertive responses can help students take more responsibility for their own learning, especially when they're involved in group projects.

- Help them be more direct in their communication, expressing clearly and concisely what they want, how they feel and what they need.

- Focus on honesty in communication.

- Help them be more empathetic toward others, to work toward understanding those with different opinions.

- Help them be persistent in their requests by, for example, clearly making eye contact when appropriate.

Guidelines for training

All that may sound straightforward enough, but it does take time and guidance. So here are some additional recommendations that can help students make assertive responses:

- Before they act, have students reflect some on the problem they are having — and develop a clear definition for themselves of what they think is wrong. They will need to understand who owns the problem. For instance, when they're confused in class but they don't ask a question, can they really expect the instructor to read their minds and intuit their needs?

- Help them plan for a preferred response. They can start by clarifying what they want. When a study group member blows off a meeting and they were counting on that person's contribution for an upcoming exam, they can think through their responses. Otherwise they may just bury their feelings under a growing pile of resentment and fear of confrontation. Help them take some initiative, doing or saying something constructive. The group will be better off for it. Their own success may be at stake. Help them be loyal to themselves, their own dreams, and those of their classmates.

- Before they attempt to put a plan into practice, however, you can help them with a visualization. Have them use their imaginations, how they think a situation would play out with different responses? If you sense their anxieties rising, back up and try again. This is exactly what desensitization programs use. If students have test anxiety, for instance, they can visualize themselves taking the exam while they practice being calm.

- Now its time to practice on others — classmates, friends, co-workers, or family members. You can have students talk a problem over in their groups, for example. There they can get support for confronting a slacker. Who knows; maybe this person will turn out to be a terrific group member if given honest feedback and the chance to respond and change. Alternatively, this person may not be ready to contribute at a level that the others want. That's okay. Everyone has choices. Everyone has responsibilities, but everyone should also be accountable.

- Finally, have them put their new plan into action and evaluate the results. Just what did happen? Are they pleased? Did they get their questions asked? Did they get their concerns addressed? Is the problem resolved? Is their group better off now? Some groups may have to experiment with various options before getting to the right "chemistry" of personalities, motivations, size, conditions, etc. Note that their skills, individually and collectively, should increase as they work together and take the time to address the effectiveness of their group.

These guidelines are not just for addressing problems, however. Students can use the same principles and practices to express appreciation to a roommate who is sensitive to their needs, to a study group member who comes on time and is ready to work, or to an instructor who puts a stimulating challenge out there for them to meet.

Remember the Robin Williams' character in the movie *Dead Poets Society*? He shows his students the "wall of honor" at Welton Academy, all those school heroes from the past. His comments went something like this:

> All these faces before you, full of hopes and dreams just like you. Full of hormones just like you. What's happened to their lives, boys? You see, they're all pushing up daisies. Food for worms, lads. Did they wait too long to make something of their lives? The Latin phrase for this is *Carpe Diem*, seize the day. Listen in boys. You can almost hear them speaking to you. Seize the day, boys. Make your lives extraordinary.

You'll remember that the film ends in a tragic suicide when one of these boys takes that big risk in opposition to a controlling father, a retired army officer with little concern for his son's feelings or dreams.

TRANSACTIONAL ANALYSIS

Another way to think about emotional intelligence is to use the ideas of Eric Berne (1964) and others (e.g., Bry, 1973; Ernst, 1973; Freed, 1971, 1973; Harris, 1969) who described communication within *Child, Adult,* and *Parent ego-states.* In a model termed Transactional Analysis, it would be the *Child* within you who can get scared or anxious and respond submissively. It can also be the *Child* within you who tries to rebel, who acts out against authority or sulks, who lashes out in anger, who reaches too quickly for a weapon. On the other end of the continuum, it may be the *Parent* within you who becomes demanding, telling others what they should or shouldn't do, controlling, or scolding them. Like those who flaunt their power or authority, this kind of response can easily move into aggressiveness. In between is the *Adult* response where you can rationally address even complex and emotionally charged issues, express yourself clearly and invite others to join you in thinking through possible solutions.

Students at all levels can find Transactional Analysis meaningful, practical, and accessible. With the use of role plays for practice, students get to examine their "ego states" in various situations, whether they have been functioning in the "Parent" mode (authoritative, caring), the "Adult" mode (rational, problem solving) or "Child" mode (spontaneous, rebellious). Having this framework in mind, then, can be useful as instructors and students alike analyze problems from the past, practice alternative strategies, and plan for the future. Understanding fighting, for example, as an expression of the "angry child" can offer a way to work toward an "adult" nonviolent alternative. After the attacks on the World Trade Center on the morning of September 11, I went into my large lecture class and attempted to use that day's topic of Transactional Analysis to offer one way of understanding the anger of the hijackers as well as the predictable anger of those wanting revenge and punishment.

Understanding Transactional Analysis can help you analyze a conflict — past, present, or expected — and think about a preferred response. For example, have you ever felt patronized by someone or talked down to? In TA terms, this might be described within the "Parent" role. Was your response to become angry? Were you, then, in the "Child" role — emotional and spontaneous? That would make sense; it's a natural response to perceived condescension. However, staying in the "Adult" role could help you break these dynamics and get to a more rational, direct, and honest basis for communication.

Along with assertiveness training, practicing Transactional Analysis can help students find alternatives to angry, violent responses. Most important, however, is how relevant these two models can be on a personal level. While many discussions about peace and nonviolence revolve around national or international issues, getting clear about constructive alternatives to violence for any of us as individuals can be profoundly important, grounding peacemaking efforts in a real, meaningful, practical, and personal context.

Chapter 7

Aligning Values
with Actions
& Thinking Ethically

Laying the groundwork for teaching and learning peace must also include a close examination of how ethical we are — how well our actions reflect our values. Bringing them in line is no easy task; and if they are not in line, we have to be willing to take action and make changes. You can tap a deep well spring of anger and frustration when core values are not in alignment with actions. For example, James Farmer (2000), one of the founders of CORE (Congress on Racial Equality) and a leader in the U.S. Civil Rights movement, noted in this essay from 1945 that a fundamental values conflict had emerged out of World War II when African American veterans returned home to find that little had changed. Despite fighting for their country, they returned to a second class citizenship or worse, a culture weighted down by the legacy of slavery and racism with very little in the way of meaningful opportunities.

Nearly a million [African American] youth have been inducted into the nation's armed forces. These men have been told that they were fighting against the theory of the "master race" and for freedom from the terrors of exploitation. That lofty aim they have in large measure accepted, though sensing an inconsistency in fighting abroad to protect for others the rights which they themselves have never enjoyed. Furthermore, their treatment, while in uniform, by their own countrymen and superior officers, has often been such as to lead them to question the war aims professed by their superiors and their government…We do not know whether the American people realize how shameful, wicked and tragic it is.…These young [African Americans] will have gone through all that other servicemen have of weariness, of danger, pain, disfigurement, horror. But in addition they will have experienced almost constant discrimination of one kind or another and frequent humiliation, and this while fighting a war allegedly fought to put an end to such a thing. (p. 170)

We want practiced what is preached. Going off to fight in World War II to stop a self-proclaimed master race meant some deep national soul searching when the returning African American veterans insisted that their country face its own racial bigotry. Muhammad Ali went to prison and lost some of his best years as a fighter when he refused induction during the Vietnam War on religious grounds, citing the hypocrisy of a war for freedom abroad when racism kept African Americans in shackles in the U.S. He offers a model of someone acting courageously on his values. His action was one of many in the 1960s that forced Americans to face the contradiction between the traditional values of democracy and the continuing practice of discrimination. In a similar manner, you can ask students to reflect on their own values and actions, to see if there might be something out of alignment that is limiting their ability to learn.

In *Savage Dreams* (1994), Rebecca Solnit describes her own experiences with aligning actions with values. Deeply concerned about the impact of nuclear weapons testing in the early 1990s on the health of the Nevada desert environment, she became involved in a series of demonstrations.

This was the place where the end of the world had been rehearsed since 1951, and it was my third spring at the camp. We

were living closer to nuclear war than anyone but its techni-
cians and its victims, which should have been devastating, but
we were doing something about it, which was heartening.
(1994, 15)

Adamantly opposed to the continued testing of nuclear weapons,
Solnit felt compelled to take some action, to join with others in a political
protest no matter the danger from proximity to the testing site.

Working with Values in the Classroom

Arriving at an ethical and moral position where we act consistently
with our values requires a process of development and growth. The book
*Values Clarification: A Handbook of Practical Strategies for Teachers and Stu-
dents* by Simon, Hart, and Kirschenbaum (1972) offers a model for working
with values that many teachers have found useful. This six-level model re-
flects a hierarchy of growth beginning with clarification and moving to
commitment and action. It builds from a very egocentric, self-referenced
position on the first level to one that emanates from deeply held "universal
ethical principles" at level six.

Level 1: Choose your values freely

Level 2: Choose from alternatives after considering the
consequences

Level 3: Prize your value choices

Level 4: Prize (affirm) your values publicly

Level 5: Act on your values

Level 6: Act repeatedly and consistently

Choosing freely

At the first stage of values clarification, Simon and his colleagues argued that we need to be able to choose freely from the options that we have.
For students, peer pressure can be fierce. How do they react when everyone
else wants to do something and they don't? Or in class, when you ask a
question and no one responds, how do you help students take some risk and
speak up? For their part, parents often exhibit significant pressure on their

children about particular career choices, especially when their parents are paying a substantial portion of the costs of college. How free do students feel to consider alternatives? Do they think through the consequences?

One way to understand student unrest in the 1960s is to recognize how the discussion about values, about civil liberties, and American ideals, in particular, hit the reality of the draft in the build-up for the Vietnam War. Young men from poor and minority communities comprised an inordinately high proportion of front line troops, an inequity that became increasingly politicized when the numbers of killed, wounded and missing in action rose. Suddenly, the actions of the government in defining U.S. interests so far away, based on core values about freedom, came home and forced an extended national debate about responsibility and sacrifice. Eventually, the deferment for college gave way to a lottery system, and the protests intensified even more.

Prizing values

Once students have thought through their feelings and beliefs, how their actions do or do not reflect their values, they can be guided to move up into the next level of this model by asking them to share their choices with others. At a personal level, for example, they can discuss their responses to disagreements and conflicts, how they manage their own anger and what that says about the values they want to hold. If you assign a group project, you can ask students to set ground rules that reflect their beliefs about communication, decision making, and equitable workloads. If current events deserve some mention, discussions can be guided toward the alignment of actions and values. For example, what does it mean for American democratic values of self-determination that the U.S. military presence is growing worldwide? Does the Patriots Act of 2002 sacrifice constitutional freedoms to keep us safe in our "war against terrorism"? As a super power, can we also be a "super cop"? Should we? At what cost to our own economy? How far should we go toward dictating what other countries should do? Should we support dictatorships when they are "friendly" to our policies? When should the United Nations be consulted? Involved? And at what cost to American autonomy or purported values when there is disagreement with that body's decisions? Is it appropriate, then, to withhold our dues?

ACTING REPEATEDLY AND CONSISTENTLY

According to the Simon et al. model, at the highest stage of values alignment you act on what you've said you believe, you "practice what you preach." Students are able to abide by the ground rules they establish for communicating about their group projects. They can hold each other accountable for agreements about workload. Clarifying all this allows them to separate what needs to happen for the group assignment from other issues — for example, from a need some may have to please others or gain acceptance. One example seen too frequently on college campuses today is where binge drinkers get trapped in their own insecurities, their desire to belong and test their new freedoms without forethought. Too often, one byproduct of such drinking and drug use is violence to self (suicide, injury) and to others (sexual assault).

At a national level, we can see a similar source of values conflict in the stories of various immigrant groups that have come to America. Ron Takaki (1993) has shifted his analyses away from a traditional accounting of demographics — populations, origins, places and dates of arrival — to focus more on the details of lives, the hopes and dreams, setbacks and struggles. Out of all of that comes a picture that is both exciting in the new opportunities that opened up as well as disturbing in the expression of racism and prejudice.

Takaki's ancestors had been recruited from Japan as cheap labor, a story common to so many immigrants coming to the U.S. Originally, they had gone to Hawaii to work on the sugar cane plantations. Despite working long, hard hours, for very little compensation, they still held onto dreams of something better for their children. Schools, then, became a focus of their hopes for a better future as well as a source of conflict over values.

> Many schools...were not preparing these children to be plantation laborers. They were learning about freedom and equality and reciting the Gettysburg Address and the Declaration of Independence. "Here the children learn about democracy or at least the theory of it," said a University of Hawaii student. They were taught that honest labor, fair play, and industriousness were virtues. But they "saw that it wasn't so on the plantation." They saw whites on the top and Asians on the bottom. Returning from school to their camps, students noticed the

wide "disparity between theory and practice." This contradiction was glaring. "The public school system perhaps without realizing it," the university student observed, "created unrest and disorganization." (p. 265)

A MORAL DEVELOPMENT MODEL

Lawrence Kohlberg (1981) postulated a theory of moral development that many teachers find useful as a model for thinking about values and the responses that students make. Although there are critiques about this model, Kohlberg's theory is still widely referenced. We can use it as a starting point here in our own deliberations on moral development.

Preconventional stage

1. Obedience. Fear of punishment.

2. Instrumental relativist. Reciprocity or what you get in return.

Conventional stage

3. Interpersonal concordance. What pleases others.

4. Maintenance of law and order.

Postconventional stage

5. Social or legalistic contract.

6. Universal ethical principles.

PRECONVENTIONAL STAGE

At **level one** in Kohlberg's model, we respond out of a *fear of punishment* or a *commitment to obedience*. For example, what stops students from fighting? Are they afraid of getting busted or do they live by some principle about personal honor and defending that honor?

At **level two**, we use what Kohlberg termed an *instrumental relativist orientation;* that is, we are concerned about *reciprocity*, what we will get back. Gang members help each other with the expectation of getting protection in return. A student might suppress his anger about someone copying from her report because she'd like to be able to call on that person for help some time in the future, perhaps when she's in a panic with too much to do in too short of a time period.

CONVENTIONAL STAGE

At **level three**, Kohlberg postulated that we reason in terms of *interpersonal concordance*, or what pleases others. New to a college campus and the surrounding community, students may be very eager to make new friends and figure out how best to fit in. That's understandable, but can it also mean that they may be susceptible to unhealthy peer pressure?

At **level four**, Kohlberg reasoned that we are concerned primarily with the maintenance of law and social order. For instance, as an instructor you might worry about the disrespect some students show in class for their instructors and classmates with their constant chatting. At this level, students might also hesitate to join a rowdy group after a big victory by the home team if they thought it might get out of hand.

POSTCONVENTIONAL

At **level five**, Kohlberg theorized that we respond according to a concern for a *social* or *legalistic contract*. We recognize that rules and laws serve social functions and that they can be altered. During the 1960s many college students joined in protesting those "Jim Crow" laws in Southern states which, for example, reserved the seating at the front of the bus for Whites or which restricted interracial marriages. Note that it was not until the late 1990s that the last of these laws was finally removed. At this level, we may consciously risk arrest, fines, and jail because we believe that a higher constitutional law protecting individual rights was being violated by local laws enforcing segregation.

At **level six**, the highest level, Kohlberg insisted that we live, act, and think according to *universal ethical principles* which we adopt after considerable thought. We do not blindly follow someone else's direction. When protesting the war in Vietnam, some idealistic students came to accept the nonviolent tenets of the great Indian leader, Mahatma Gandhi and were willing to risk jail because of their opposition to the war.

QUESTIONS ABOUT KOHLBERG

Critics have challenged several aspects of this model: the focus on ethics at the top of Kohlberg's model, the cultural context (Western, male, Anglo), the nature of the stages themselves and their relationships to each other. With these cautions in mind, this theory can nonetheless be helpful as a vehicle for assessing — and challenging — anyone's thinking.

When discussing the issue of *political correctness* — for example, that we must support the President in times of war or that valuing nonviolence in the face of terror is weakness — less mature students may respond in terms of perceived effects, such as the consequences of being criticized by an instructor for expressing unpopular views (stage 1) or the benefits of popularity with peers by agreeing with the majority (stage 3). Teachers, in turn, may miss all this and overestimate how students will think, perhaps assuming that the class is following a free and more principled inquiry (stage 6). Knowing about Kohlberg's hierarchy can help us better understand these kinds of dynamics, allowing for more thoughtful reflection and self-assessment.

However, there is more here. Having defined the levels of moral development, Kohlberg then went one step further and theorized that students may not be able to understand reasoning more than one level above their own stage of thinking. If he was right about this, traditional instruction may indeed miss the mark at times. Highly principled comments may, unfortunately, fall on deaf (cognitively blocked) ears. We may be talking over the heads of our audiences.

THE GENDER QUESTION – CAROL GILLIGAN

In her provocative book, *In a Different Voice*, Carol Gilligan (1982), a former member of the Kohlberg research effort, has raised some fundamental questions about the universality of several developmental models, arguing that the works of Piaget, Kohlberg, and others may, in fact, have predictive value primarily for white males living in Western societies. While analyzing research protocols, Gilligan ran into difficulty as she attempted to categorize female responses within Kohlberg's hierarchy.

According to Gilligan, young females consistently utilized reasoning that did not clearly fit anywhere within Kohlberg's model. Many of her subjects wanted to talk about relationships and how these would be affected by particular decisions. Whereas males tended to argue about legalistic and ethical considerations, females often worried about the effects of a particular decision on others. With respect to fighting, for example, females might worry more about the damage this could do to the relationship between two students than who was right and who should be punished.

AN EVOLUTIONARY PROCESS

Kohlberg's model and Gilligan's critique demonstrate that the moral and ethical growth necessary to consistently align values with action is an evolutionary process. Martin Luther King, Jr.'s life offers an excellent example here. As the war in Vietnam intensified and its costs stretched the federal budget, President Johnson's promises about a "war on poverty" to redress basic inequities, barriers, and grievances were gradually undermined. As war protestors called into question the government's morality, King recognized a deeper rift between our values and actions. This recognition led him to expand the focus of his work on civil rights to include a critique of the capitalistic economic system and the war in Vietnam.

> [In] all his speeches, King's voice was heard calling for what he described as "a revolution in values" in the United States, a struggle to free ourselves form the "triple evils of racism, extreme materialism, and militarism."...By the end of the fall (of 1967), King's voice...was setting forth a jarring theme, declaring, "Something is wrong with capitalism as it now stands in the United States. We are not interested in being integrated into *this* value structure. Power must be relocated....We've got to make it known that until our problem is solved, America may have many, many days, but they will be full of trouble. There will be no rest, there will be no tranquility in this country until the nation comes to terms with our problems. (Harding, 2000, pp. 198-199)

Part II: Tools, Models, & Methods

This section connects the values and models of Part I with specific classroom teaching strategies, models, and methods — it offers tools and ideas for applying the concepts explored in Part I in the classroom. I have always felt it important to explore new possibilities in an active, hands-on manner so that I can challenge my assumptions and continue my own learning. The process of planning, implementation, assessment, and reflection can help us rethink what may have become too comfortable and consider new ways to approach the challenges we face.

Chapter 8

Instructional Strategies that Reinforce Teaching Peace

Discovery Learning

As we continue to discuss the implications of September 11, we need more integrative and interdisciplinary thinking to adequately address all those conditions that gave rise to the attacks as well as what responses will have a long-term, sustainable, and restorative impact. In the opening section to *Earth in Mind,* David Orr (1994) addresses the preoccupation of education with acquired knowledge, ordered and sequenced within disciplinary boundaries and its cost to the kind of thinking that is essential for confronting complex problems in the real world.

> We have fragmented the world into bits and pieces called disciplines and subdisciplines, hermetically sealed from other such disciplines. As a result, after 12 or 16 or 20 years of education, most students graduate without any broad, integrated

sense of the unity of things. The consequences for their personhood and for the planet are large. For example, we routinely produce economists who lack the most rudimentary understanding of ecology or thermodynamics. This explains why our national accounting systems do not subtract the costs of biotic impoverishment, soil erosion, poisons in our air and water, and resource depletion from gross national product. (1994, 11)

Beyond a need for reorganization, David Orr goes on to argue for rethinking the very way in which education is delivered and assessed — or, in other words, *how* we teach can be as important as *what* we teach.

Process is important for learning. Courses taught as lecture courses tend to induce passivity. Indoor classes create the illusion that learning only occurs inside four walls, isolated from what students call, without apparent irony, the "real world."…Campus architecture is crystallized pedagogy that often reinforces passivity, monologue, domination, and artificiality. My point is simply that students are being taught in various and subtle ways beyond the overt content of courses. (1994, 14)

Discovery learning is designed to engage students as active participants in the pursuit of knowledge, allowing them to confront a puzzle, a problem, or a challenge, and to follow their own lead towards a solution. It has much in common with higher education's research mission. Instead of asking students to demonstrate their mastery of existing facts and theories, we ask them to turn their attention, creativity, and intelligence toward problems and issues that have no known immediate answer or solution. It is in this cauldron of possibilities that students can best begin to think critically and independently.

However, for learning to occur, students must be willing to take initiative. You are challenging them. Instead of listening passively as you describe a problem and the challenges of finding a solution, your students have to respond to your challenge and explore possibilities. They may have to respond to questions, search the published literature on a subject, conduct experiments, or some other form of systematic investigation. With its emphasis on active engagement, discovery learning allows students to experience what Bruner (1966) called "the process of knowledge-getting." This approach taps their energies, experiences, and inner resources in new and different ways.

Suchman (1962) called this approach "inquiry training" and emphasized the empowerment which comes when students know better how to approach a problem, formulate questions, and generate plausible solutions for themselves. Joyce and Weil (2000) described the basic premises and benefits of this approach.

- We inquire naturally when we are puzzled;

- We can become more conscious of our own thinking (metacognition);

- We can learn new strategies to aid in reflection and discovery;

- We can utilize cooperative inquiry to enrich our thinking, to understand the tentative, emergent nature of knowledge, and to appreciate alternative explanations.

DISCOVERY ACROSS THE DISCIPLINES

Despite the popularity of the lecture, a variety of subjects, courses and contexts lend themselves readily to a discovery approach. In the science laboratory, the art studio, the music practice room, and the theater, for example, students can explore their own insights or interpretations as their studies progress. Learning is grounded here in tangible, concrete reality — in the chemicals, equipment, and procedures of a science experiment; in the clay or wood of a sculpture; in brushes and paint; in a musical instrument or score; in the text, props, and set of a theater production. Efforts to develop peacemaking can also build from activities that require direct involvement, teamwork, and the use of good communication skills.

In any class, open-ended questions can trigger student curiosity. A problem can focus their attention. By building off compelling issues that arouse student interests and tap their idealism, we can help them apply what they're learning in meaningful ways. As an intellectual activity, discovery taps a variety of abilities, both intellectual and emotional. Students learn to pool their knowledge and hunches as they explore possible solutions. They learn how to confront a range of ideas and opinions, to test and compare different answers, and to make inferences based upon multiple perspectives. By designing lessons that incorporate some of life's uncertainties — for example, the dangers inherent in violent and aggressive responses — we give students a chance to experience some of what any scholar faces on the frontiers of knowledge.

For a discovery lesson to be successful, you and your students will need a certain intellectual and emotional *readiness*. Collectively, your curiosity and willingness to explore ideas and possibilities drive the process. However, you should also be prepared for some degree of unpredictability. That is very important. Frustration and anxiety are common. These emotions can be problematic; they can *also* be useful prods for learning. Many students are successful because they give instructors exactly what is expected. When that kind of prescribed instruction gives way to a discovery lesson, you face your students with very new and different challenges. For example, Rowe (1974) stresses the importance of "wait time" in response to questions. Too often, we underestimate the time required for students to think about questions and begin to formulate their responses. Lowman (1995) suggests that once students become familiar with some silence, participation will usually increase and long waits became rare.

Assessment

Discovery assignments often challenge instructors to broaden their expectations of student capabilities and needs. Ironically, those students who are thought to be among the "best" in class — those who complete assignments on time, who come to class prepared, participate actively in class discussions, and score well on traditional measures of learning — may struggle when called upon to analyze a problem on their own and then develop and test various hypotheses. Conversely, students who may be bored with the routine of listening and note-taking can come to life when challenged by a discovery lesson. Throughout the process, cooperative groups (discussed in the third section of this chapter) can prove valuable for students who experience difficulty or need the support of others to take risks.

Because the exploration can be lively, interesting, and fun for everyone, there may be more confusion, frustration, and noise in class during a discovery lesson. The benefits can be well worth these hassles, especially when you and your students learn how to deal positively with the unpredictability inherent in the process.

BALANCING CAUTION AND ACTION

While discovery remains central to the role and mission of universities, in particular, there is always a shadow side, aspects that are problematic. For example, when should "scientific advances" be questioned? Resisted? And when should new discoveries move beyond analyses and into action? The corollary to this question is also important to discovery learning — how long should action be delayed in the case of discoveries that seem intuitively correct but are not yet scientifically proven. The "Precautionary Principle" — evolved from discussions at the 1992 United Nations Conference on Environment and Development in Rio de Janero, Brazil — argues that certain precautionary measures should be taken in cases where an incompletely proven discovery would be clearly beneficial and where a scientifically-based discovery has proven harmful. For example, existing environmental regulations, based on some of the most advanced scientific thinking, have "failed to protect adequately human health" or the "larger system of which humans are but a part....Therefore, it is necessary to implement the 'Precautionary Principle.' When an activity raises threats of harm to human health or the environment, precautionary measures should be taken even if some cause and effect relationships are not fully established" (Holdridge, 2000, 17).

For example, we don't know the exact nature of the relationship between treaties to limit nuclear weapons testing and our collective security. However, many of us believe that such agreements are important for maintaining peace among the nuclear powers. The treaties are precautionary measures that should be taken even though some people claim there is no "proof" they will work. Likewise, we may not know the exact nature of the relationship between easy access to handguns in the U.S. and our historically high rates of murder, but we should take precautions despite the claims by the gun lobby that no relationship has been proven.

On the other hand, caution about the uncertainties of some discoveries is still necessary, even if the discoveries are "scientifically based." The usefulness of our degrees often erodes because new information frequently disproves old discoveries. I have heard, for example, that the "shelf-life" of an engineering degree is three to five years unless updated. If discoveries of new knowledge change our thinking over time, how can we best help students remain appropriately cautious about what they are learning today, as well as appropriately willing to take precautionary measures when discoveries are intuitively valid but still unproven?

INDUCTIVE THINKING

Other mechanisms for analyzing puzzling or complex issues can help us arrive at new interpretations. Scholars and scientists from very different fields regularly use an inductive approach — and its process of moving from the particular to the general — to help them work toward conclusions. For his popular book, *The Seasons of a Man's Life*, psychologist Dan Levinson interviewed men in different careers and noticed that certain patterns emerged across the life span. Gail Sheehy's *Passages* and Levinson's subsequent book with his wife Judy, *The Seasons of a Woman's Life,* which built on new data from females of different ages and careers, offered additional and somewhat different interpretations. Scholars such as Piaget, Erikson, Bruner, Belenky, Perry, Rogoff, Tharp and Gallimore have also made use of the inductive process to generalize about patterns that develop over time.

The inductive process involves data gathering, grouping, labeling, developing, and testing hypotheses. To demonstrate the steps of the inductive process, we can revisit Solnit's experiences with the issue of nuclear testing. In *Savage Dreams* (1994), she wondered about the loss of public interest in the early 1990's around nuclear weapons testing. It was happening at a time when the explosive power of these bombs had become far greater than what was dropped by the U.S. on Hiroshima and Nagasaki toward the end of World War II. Here she describes a series of protests and the ensuing public reaction:

> By the end of the ten-day event in 1988, 2,000 people had been arrested from among the 5,000 participants — and no charges were pressed in the vast majority of the cases. It was one of the biggest civil disobedience arrests in U.S. history, and it barely made the local news. In 1988, [most of] the nuclear bombs exploded at the Test Site...ranged from 20 to 150 kilotons as did 1989s bombs....They didn't make the news either. (1994, 27-28)

Recall that in World War II, Hiroshima had been laid waste with a 15 kiloton bomb and Nagasaki with 21 kilotons. Then, why so little public reaction in the late 1980s? The bombs being tested in 1988 were much bigger, the protests were sizable, lots of people were getting arrested, and yet, there was very little public response. Let's look at this dilemma using the steps of the inductive process.

1. Organize the data: What do we know? What are the facts? Lots of protesters and lots of arrests. Lots of large test bombs exploded. No evidence here of excessive use of force by the police. In most cases, no formal charges were filed.

2. Group the data: What information goes together? What was it that the authorities did? The protesters? Those in charge of the bomb tests? The news media?

3. Label these groupings: One possible grouping of these data could include events surrounding the arrests, how the authorities decided to handle those kinds of numbers on the scene and how they handled subsequent events when formal charges had to be filed. Another grouping might include information about the bombs detonated, the numbers, and sizes, and how these fit with previous tests, existing treaties, etc. Another could include information about the relationship between reporting of demonstrations and the success of the protesters in reaching the public.

4. Develop hypotheses about the interrelationships among these groupings: Were the media and the public tired of the issue? Would the demonstrators need some "police brutality" to get more attention? Was it a conscious choice of the authorities to handle the protesters with minimal force and no arrests, despite the trespassing laws being broken? Would crowded jails and clogged court dockets have created more havoc than bending the letter of the law and letting the demonstrators go free? Was the warming of the Cold War allowing Americans to turn their attention elsewhere? Or was the media encouraged to downplay the protest?

5. Test your ideas, reevaluate and rethink the entire process: Solnit offers various insights about the viability of these guesses. However, as a reader, you can't blindly accept what Solnit — or anyone else — concludes without your own independent evaluation of the

events and interpretations offered. Eventually, you can return to your original guesses and reevaluate the way you looked at the problem in the first place. What other data should you consider? What new questions arise in your own mind? One big advantage students have is the opportunity to raise questions in class and hear from others. As instructors we can acknowledge sound reasoning even if we disagree with a student's conclusions.

Alternate interpretations and conclusions

People with different mind sets can analyze the data and come up with very different conclusions. For example, how do you think Martin Luther King, Jr. would assess today's world? Where would he be hopeful? Despondent? In "My Pilgrimage to Nonviolence" (King, 2000), he looked back over the first half of the twentieth century. In doing so, he could have concluded the worst from all the wars and conflicts worldwide. Instead, he chose to frame the historical record from a different perspective, one of hope. Looking back, do we see King's assessment as unrealistically naïve or a tangible sign of his genius? How do we judge an optimism that is grounded in possibility, articulating an achievable though distant goal and energizing others through difficult times?

> We who live in the twentieth century are privileged to live in one of the most momentous periods of human history. It is an exciting age, filled with hope. It is an age in which a new social order is being born. We stand today between two worlds — the dying old and the emerging new. Now I am aware of the fact that there are those who would contend that we live in the most ghastly period of human history. They would argue that the rhythmic beat of the deep rumblings of discontent from Asia, the uprisings in Africa, the nationalistic longings of Egypt, the roaring cannons from Hungary, and the racial tensions of America are all indicative of the deep and tragic midnight which encompasses our civilization. They would argue that we are retrogressing instead of progressing. But far from representing retrogression and tragic meaninglessness, the present tensions represent the necessary pains that accompany the birth of anything new. (2000, 178)

A caution

Like most things in life, however, there are cautions associated with the inductive process. For instance, someone could come up with conclusions that are unreasonable, unsupportable. A student might look at a poor grade and jump too quickly to pin the blame on a professor or the book, unwilling to accept any personal responsibility. In *Something in the Soil,* Historian Patricia Limerick (2000, 36) warns about the too easy conclusions that oversimplify — and thereby mythologize — complex events.

> In graduate school, we were trained to be finders of themes. Where others might see a bunch of unconnected facts, we were obligated to locate the underlying patterns. And, unlike many exercises, this one was addictive. In a world so overloaded with complexity and contradiction, the activity of getting a grip on themes and patterns is genuinely comforting and soothing. This ability of generalizations to bring calm is particularly appealing when one confronts ugly forms of human behavior.

Limerick wants to debunk a specific oversimplification here. In your own early school years, you undoubtedly read about the "Indian wars" in the West that marked the movement of European settlers, prospectors, traders, and troops across North America. Limerick notes that the "idea of an Indian war as a conflict of whites against Indians seldom had much to do with reality because Indians were usually on both sides of the conflict" (p. 47). As with all concepts or definitions, we must stay open to new interpretations based on reanalyses. A full understanding of the violence from the past can help us better understand the present in all its rich and, too often, frustrating complexity.

Cooperative Learning

As educators, there is much we can learn from the way cooperation has been effectively used for large and meaningful efforts in the real world. For example, Argentina's Adolfo Perez Esquivel was awarded the 1980 Nobel Peace Prize for his courageous and tireless work coordinating Servicio Paz y Justicia (Service for Peace and Justice), an organization dedicated to nonviolent social change and human rights protections in Latin America. Despite widespread harassment, persecution, imprisonment, and killings — the response of repressive and military dictatorships to any dissent — Esquivel and his colleagues have eschewed any armed retaliation. At the heart of their effort has been a core commitment to the cooperation necessary to bring diverse viewpoints to the table for meaningful discussions and reconciliation. Yet, those are only their short-term goals, for at the core has also been a commitment to addressing widespread inequities as a necessary foundation for sustainable peace in the region.

> Bishops, priests, pastors and laypeople were seeking a "way of liberation" consonant with the gospel; situations of injustice were clamoring for attention. Efforts — often limited and isolated — to bring about change nonviolently were being made; there was a need for coordination, communication, and collaboration among persons and groups concerned for nonviolent change....Because of this reality of the systematic, widespread, and prolonged violation of human rights, Servicio was led to make human rights a principal program emphasis which was Latin American in scope and won worldwide interest and support. It was while active in that effort that Adolfo was arrested in April 1977 and imprisoned without charges for fourteen months, after which he spent another fourteen months in "restricted freedom." (Chartier 2000, 100)

In the context of an increasingly interdependent world, cooperative groups represent one way for you to teach peacemaking at a skill level that is both practical and meaningful, where students work together to achieve common goals, assisting and supporting each other's learning while resolving issues that arise along the way. As an instructor, you also get to interact with them in their small groups on more of a personal scale. By grouping individuals with different abilities, backgrounds, and viewpoints, you can encourage more diverse perspectives to surface as well as create a more diverse context for the use of the skills discussed in Chapter 5 ("Establishing Communication") — the skills of listening, expressing empathy, and seeking consensus. A diversity of perspectives and the skills that make diversity workable are essential for a vibrant society and a healthy democracy. When managed effectively, groups can provide a kind of classroom laboratory for the development of critical and creative thinking (Timpson and Bendel-Simso 1996).

Learning groups also represent a powerful alternative to the traditional lecture format. By augmenting large class meetings with small cooperative group activities, you can share some of the responsibility for instruction with students and shift authority from a strict hierarchy to one that is more participatory and co-creative. Solutions and conclusions are not just imposed from on high. For example, student groups can assume some control over a particular domain of the curriculum. They can research certain topics, prepare reports, and make presentations in class. You *do* give up some class time and the quality of student presentations can vary. However, these kinds of cooperative projects can be very important for students, their learning and development.

Active learning

Cooperative groups require that students engage actively with course material. The learning process becomes more individualized as students interact with their classmates in ways which are personally meaningful, offering ideas, listening, to the others, reaching for agreement, dividing up responsibilities, checking on progress, attempting to resolve differences and tensions. A learning group is also a place where students can speak about ideas they do not yet fully understand. By sharing, listening and reflecting in this smaller and less threatening environment, they can become more aware of their own thinking and beliefs.

Students can also discover what they *don't* know. Unlike the lecture format, where instructors present information in a sequential and orderly manner, group learning can help students identify their own intellectual blind spots, where their thinking may be unformed, flawed, or confused. Collaborative projects can encourage them to experiment with ideas and eventually deepen their understanding of core concepts, integrating new material into a more meaningful, coherent, and defensible system. With this kind of *constructivist* learning, students make new information their own.

The idea of cooperative *action* has long been important to the peace movement. Despite its seeming inactivity, even pacifism requires focused clarity and real courage to defend. In truth, pacifism has been difficult for many to accept in the face of hostile threats, such as the rise of Hitler and Fascism. One of Martin Luther King Jr.'s most important insights — as described in a 1958 piece called "My Pilgrimage to Nonviolence" — came when he realized how active Gandhi meant nonviolent resistance to be. The "other cheek" would not be meekly turned when slapped. Instead, a campaign would be mounted to appeal to a higher moral code of behavior and shame the aggressor.

> My study of Gandhi convinced me that true pacifism is not non-resistance to evil, but nonviolent resistance to evil. Between the two positions, there is a world of difference. Gandhi resisted evil with as much vigor and power as the violent resistor, but he resisted with love instead of hate. True pacifism is not unrealistic submission to evil power…It is rather a courageous confrontation of evil by the power of love, in the faith that it is better to be the recipient of violence than the inflictor of it, since the latter only multiplied the existence of violence and bitterness in the universe, while the former may develop a sense of shame in the opponent and thereby bring about a transformation and change of heart. (King 2000, p. 69)

COGNITIVE AND AFFECTIVE OUTCOMES

The peace movement has often focused on raising public awareness, on building support and influencing policy makers through rallies, petition drives, teach-ins, and the like. In *the classroom*, David and Roger Johnson (1994) have reminded us of the parallel power of cooperative learning. In the cognitive domain, they can point to thirty years of research demonstrating the superiority of group learning across a wide range of factors: for mastery of concepts and principles, for enhanced verbal abilities, problem-solving skills, reasoning, creative thinking, and general self-awareness as well as for an improved ability to view ideas in proper perspective. By engaging actively with factual information, concepts or principles, they claim that students in groups can show an increased ability to retain, apply, and transfer new knowledge. In addition, students can develop democratic values and a greater acceptance and appreciation of individual differences. Conflict resolution and peacemaking certainly draw on these same skills and abilities.

The Johnsons also claim that when groups function well, interpersonal communication will improve. With some guidance on your part, students can use their groups as mini-labs for learning how to listen and express themselves better, how to address problems, negotiate, and reach consensus. Leadership abilities can develop. The involvement of group members often produces more varied input, and here diversity can provide a distinct advantage. As students from different backgrounds contribute, discussions can expand and deepen. Better and more creative decisions can result. Without these kinds of cooperative experiences, of reaching across divisions, it is easy to see how isolated and antagonistic groups, whether inside or outside schools, will only deepen their dislike for each other and sharpen their differences.

FLEXIBILITY OF GROUPS

Learning groups are appealing in part because they offer a broad range of possibilities. Depending on your goals, group size may vary, although five to seven members seems best for maximizing participation. The length of time you devote to any group activity can also vary. You may decide to incorporate a short activity as a change of pace within the context of a lecture or introduce a collaborative assignment that lasts the entire class period. In large classes where seats are bolted down, you can have students consult with others seated nearby or assign projects to be pursued for the most part outside of class time. Weekly assignments or term projects can also be organized cooperatively. Because students are often busy, you may have to help them get their groups started: for example, you can schedule a time and place for those who want to form study groups. You can also use email as a mechanism for linking students outside of class. These kinds of experiences help build the networking skills we all need to fully participate in the democratic process.

For some cooperative projects it is possible to divide the labor so that group members take responsibility for learning material or developing skills individually before coming back together to contribute to the whole. This technique, often used by students in study groups to manage their time more efficiently, has been dubbed the *jigsaw* because each participant contributes an essential piece to the completed puzzle. This also helps develop skills useful in peacemaking. As noted in the example of Esquivel and Servicio, in order to be effective, nonviolent efforts at social justice in the face of oppressive controls and persecution typically require many people doing many different things.

A good way to show students how the "jigsaw" approach can work is to use it as a way to help them prepare for an upcoming exam. After dividing course material into comparable sections, ask each member of a group to take responsibility for a particular subset of readings, notes, etc. You, then, ask them to meet in new groups around their particular subsets to explore what's essential. When the original groups reassemble, each member has a critical role to play apprising others of key concepts and study hints from his or her particular part. There is usually high participation, effective sharing, and genuine group bonding during this kind of structured review period. Because there is a lot at stake, a mutual interdependence develops quickly. Once students experience the benefits here, they may be more likely to continue their cooperative studies outside of class. Harnessing these student resources and nurturing their feeling of responsibility toward each other can create a powerful *infrastructure* for learning in your classes.

The instructor's role

Admittedly, collaborative learning has its own inherent challenges and complexities. Bouton and Rice (1983) point out that the success of individual students in mastering course content correlates positively with the quality of the interaction taking place among members of the group. Using group learning, however, does not mean abdicating your responsibility; rather, you shift your focus toward designing and managing activities where students can be active in supporting each other's understanding. Michaelsen (1983) describes the tasks facing teachers who choose to use learning groups. They include:

- forming the groups;
- building and maintaining group cohesiveness;
- sequencing instructional activities;
- organizing material;
- developing and managing group-oriented classroom activities;
- evaluating performance;
- providing feedback.

In all of this, your role as manager of the group experience is vital. To do this well will take some time. If you are used to more traditional lecturing, you may need to develop a different set of skills for effective group facilitation. For example, you will want to monitor groups closely so that workloads are distributed fairly and all students contribute to the collective effort. Some groups may require regular supervision in order to stay on task. You may also have to watch out for "collaborative" misinformation where incorrect "solutions" are passed around unchecked.

As for assessment, most instructors who use cooperative learning establish mechanisms for measuring individual and group progress. If you decide to assign a group grade, you can expect a mixed response from students: on one hand, they will typically appreciate the support and assistance they receive from other group members. On the other hand, they do not want to be held hostage to slackers who fail to follow through on their promises. Ask your better students, in particular, about their experiences in groups and you will often hear their frustration about feeling exploited. While this anxiety can create tensions within groups, it can also promote greater effort and enhance performance, both collectively and individually. Good communication skills as well as a sound understanding of group processes can make even difficult situations a viable laboratory for meaningful learning.

When the time comes to evaluate a project, it is a good idea to require group members to evaluate their own performance. After assuring students that the information they provide will be kept confidential, ask them to identify positive aspects of the group experience, individuals or situations which were problematic, and what insights or recommendations they can offer. In addition, you might try requiring students to maintain a journal where they can explore their own reactions to this assignment and, thereby, develop greater awareness about group process. All of this information can help you fine tune your future use of the group-learning format.

IMPACT ON STUDENTS

Because group assignments provide valuable support and assistance for individual group members, they can empower students to assume greater responsibility for their own learning. Through interdependence, they can learn to communicate more effectively with peers, to work efficiently with others, to define a task, to divide up labor, to resolve conflict,s and more. The mutual support students experience can encourage risk-taking, another quality that supports learning.

Well-managed group projects can also contribute to a sense of community and camaraderie, resulting in a general boost in morale for students and teachers. Apathy, absenteeism, and poor performance often decline. In a similar vein, Maimon (1983) recommends collaborative groups as a means to overcome the isolation and loneliness experienced by graduate students, particularly in the humanities. Unlike science students, who commonly work in groups in the laboratory, students in other disciplines often spend many solitary hours in the library. At the undergraduate level, students may become isolated for different reasons. Tobias (1992), for example, notes that many talented students often report feeling discouraged in large introductory science classes which are information driven, graded competitively on a curve and, accordingly, are inherently isolating.

Students unfamiliar with the group approach or unskilled in basic communication may face difficulties and frustration initially. Individuals with a strong preference for independent learning, for example, may really struggle within this format. Others may feel frustrated when their inability to explain themselves, understand others, or negotiate differences proves problematic. While David and Roger Johnson encourage the use of heterogeneous groupings so that the diverse abilities needed for success are built into every group, unsuccessful projects can highlight these differences. If conflicts do arise among group members, you can help students by actively teaching the requisite social skills needed for effective teamwork. Individuals and groups often need guidance in learning to work together effectively. In this period when conflicts regularly impact every level of society and periodically threaten to explode into violence, cooperative academic experiences can provide essential and powerful lessons about learning and peaceful change.

Alternating instructional strategies

Indeed, learning groups are rapidly taking their place alongside the lecture and the discussion as a popular mode of instruction in higher education. Finkel and Monk (1983) point to the varying functions of a teacher and how these can be shared with students. They recommend that you distinguish among three course components: course activities (teaching, practicing, experiencing, grading); those people responsible for performing the course activities (you, teaching assistants, graders); and the places (times, rooms) where these activities occur. Once you have made this analysis, you can then choose among the various options so as to maximize students' learning. For example, when can students give feedback to each other and augment what you yourself can provide? When can you ask them to present? As you experiment with instructional strategies, Finkel and Monk add, it is essential that you and your students remain clear about the boundaries separating one function from another since behavior and expectations vary within each format.

MY EXPERIENCE WITH COOPERATIVE LEARNING

In my own classes, I have experimented with many variations of group learning, yet I try to stay alert to new possibilities. I've seen the benefits of building a supportive and positive class climate. I see students as invaluable resources for instruction and learning. They can provide each other with different perspectives, feedback, and assistance far beyond what I could ever hope to give as one individual. Of course, I do need to manage the process with some foresight, care, and attention, especially to the precision (concepts, definitions, theories) that the content may require.

For example, I commonly require a group project where students, both undergraduate and graduate, must work together to plan, develop, rehearse, facilitate, and then evaluate a learning experience for their classmates. A group grade quickly welds individual students into a functioning team. While I find that I must provide some active guidance for these groups as their planning unfolds, giving over some class time to the process, I am invariably rewarded — and my classes enriched — as students bring a wonderful blend of energy, variety, and creativity with their presentations.

At other times, I have had students cooperate in completing a group exam question. While individual contributions are difficult to tease apart, the intensity and depth of the interactions make this a viable learning option. I do track individual performance along the way, but nothing promotes interdependence like a group grade. In the debriefing process that I always like to hold, I discuss with students what happened, the perceived advantages and problems, how different people reacted, and what they could do differently the next time. I like to think that I am contributing to the students developing vital skills with lifelong benefits.

I have also organized cooperative in-class study sessions, where I subdivide a class and have certain students work together to master particular content. I then reorganize the class into other groups in such a way that all the material will be covered. In this way, each student becomes an expert and vital to his or her group's overall success. One important advantage to this approach is the potential extension where students carry this benefit outside of class and initiate their own study groups. Light (1992), for example, has reported remarkable benefits, especially in demanding science classes, for students who naturally find others for study outside of class. Using cooperative study groups in class helps many students who might otherwise work independently take those important first steps towards developing their collaborative skills.

When I ask students to evaluate a course at the end of a semester, the various group activities usually receive top marks. Students often report feeling empowered, proud of what their groups accomplished. They have been active in constructing meaning for themselves and their classmates. Many will also report having made some good new friends.

I have also found that group learning provides a microcosm of challenges that indeed mirrors what society demands. Whether in work settings or in the home, in professional, public, or personal arenas, the ability to work effectively with others, to communicate across differences, and tap the creative synergy inherent in diversity becomes an essential base for any efforts at peacemaking and conflict resolution. I could see this dynamic operating during the teach-ins we organized on campus after September 11. New conversations occurred across fields. Historians, sociologists, political scientists, educators, economists, and philosophers joined with students, community members, representatives of various religious groups, and others to share their expertise, experiences, and insights.

Chapter 9

Empowerment
through Performance

Jesuit priest Daniel Berrigan made headlines with his brother Phillip and others staging protests during the Vietnam War. Convinced that the war was immoral, the Berrigans used a range of strategies to create the kinds of memorable events that would attract the attention of the media and the public. Given the power and resources of governments to control the news, the inertia that blocks change as well as the general apathy, it is easy to see why activists would gravitate toward the dramatic. Here Dan Berrigan describes their tactics at the Pentagon:

> Our purpose there was to bring home to the authorities the meaning and consequences of their decisions to build and sell weapons around the world thus depriving the poor of life and the right use of the world. We used, as is usual in our efforts, a range of ways of communicating. Some distribute leaflets and carry on conversation with Pentagon employees. Some wear costumes and play the parts of specters of death, walking through the Pentagon concourses, the acres of shops and restaurants and banks beneath the military offices, chanting 'death, death, death, the bomb, the bomb, the bomb." Still others poured blood, our own blood, which earlier had been gathered clinically by a nurse in the group. The blood was poured

out on pillars, walls, doorways, the floor — a terrific amount of blood dripping everywhere. And ashes were poured as well: a sign of our readiness to burn the living. A number of people fell as if dead into the blood and ashes. We carried a cross on which the names of various weapons had been written: Trident, cruise missile, neutron bomb, nuclear warhead, napalm…all the machinery of death. (Berrigan 2000, 95)

Whenever you are facing the big issues of war and peace, violence and reconciliation, you may need to step outside of what's conventional to get noticed and be heard. The theater has long been a source of inspiration for engaging audiences and telling stories in compelling ways. In *Teaching and Performing,* Suzanne Burgoyne and I, described the many ways that instructors can use "lessons from the stage" to energize their teaching and stimulate a deeper learning.

At the top of any list on teaching effectiveness…should be student learning. To be successful…requires much more than subject matter expertise. It requires some mastery of delivery — especially in large classes — as well as some skill in engaging the minds and hearts of students, in challenging them to consider new possibilities and rethink old ideas. (2002, 2-3)

Current trends in higher education point toward the use of approaches that actively engage students and challenge them to think more critically and creatively (see Davis, 1993; Eble, 1994; Johnson, Johnson & Smith, 1989; Johnson & Johnson, 1994; Lowman, 1995; McKeachie, 2002; Ramsden, 1992; Timpson & Bendel-Simso, 1996).

Some of your students, however, may be quite complacent about their own learning, comfortable with the status quo, enmeshed in what Freire (1970) termed the *banking* notion of education. In this more traditional but enduring practice, teachers attempt to get "deposits" of information into the minds of the young. During this process, instructors socialize students into a receptive but, Freire argued, fundamentally dysfunctional culture of silence and passivity. Here education and learning of a certain type can reinforce student docility and conventional ways of thinking.

The national literacy campaigns that sprang out of Paulo Freire's work in Central America, South America and Africa are examples of the value of more active and empowering models of education, where teachers moved away from a conventional focus on information-giving and toward a facilitated learning process. When I visited Cuba, Nicaragua and Brazil to see these efforts first hand, I understood better how poor and illiterate masses literally "bootstrapped" themselves upward by means of involvement in small, interactive study groups facilitated by volunteers who mixed their own limited reading ability with enthusiasm, commitment and idealism. A desire to read was built on student stories — oral descriptions of their own life experiences, concerns, hopes and dreams — and, then, transformed slowly, word by word and sentence by sentence, into an understanding of written language (see Timpson, 1988). Throughout Freire's work is the imperative that teachers foster engagement through the use of meaningful material, that they avoid information giving or "banking," and that they stay committed to their facilitator's *role*.

Out of these successes with literacy and empowerment emerged a very original adaptation to the theater that holds much promise for peace education. After the publication of Freire's (1970) classic, *Pedagogy of the Oppressed,* Augusto Boal (1979, 1992, 1995) began to explore its application to the theater and later wrote *Theater of the Oppressed,* among other books. Here he described various ways in which actors can use the lived experiences of audience members to generate material for the "stage." Every performance would be fresh and meaningful to the audience that is present. There are no written scripts to portray, just what the actors can coax from those in attendance. The struggles, challenges, hopes, and dreams of audience members themselves become the focus for improvisations. Scenes are "acted out" by actors (used primarily to jump start a scene) and recruits from the audience. Whoever volunteered the issue gets to see other perspectives and possibilities.

Using the ideas of Freire and the techniques of Augusto Boal, a lesson on peace education and nonviolence might look like the following: First, students (or any audience members for that matter) are invited to suggest problems for the group. According to Boal, these should be real and complex. With everyone's input, new and different solutions will be explored in a variety of ways. For example, someone might want to work on a conflicted relationship that threatens to turn violent. Someone else might be outraged at a new movie's graphic violence and want some ideas about staging a protest. A parent might want to help a child use nonviolent alternatives to confront a bully at school. An instructor could want to have better communication in class when issues like affirmative action and white privilege spark strong feelings and defensive reactions.

Once underway, the students who bring up the "issue" or "problem" choose individuals to play particular roles. They might pick some to be "students" and someone to be the "instructor." The "scene" would be set and the action begun. Note that having participation from people with some acting experience can be helpful to get things going. At any point, however, anyone from the audience can yell, "STOP" and jump into any of the roles. After each run through you want to ask the person with the issue: "What was new? Was it believable? What did you learn?" Again, the goal is to give the person with the issue multiple and different perspectives, new possibilities. The action is usually fast so you have to make sense of it all on the fly. Everyone gets involved. The audience is the cast and crew.

Another Boal technique is to use *sculpting* to see an issue from a physical, nonverbal perspective. People are recruited from the audience to play various "statues" in a scene that captures the essence of a particular problem. For example, someone wants to stage a protest of an extremely violent film at a local movie theater — think of the controversy surrounding *Natural Born Killers*. In a first sculpture, people might be positioned as the film's killers and their victims. Others are positioned as audience members — terrified, eating popcorn, wide eyed. Once in place, everyone has a few moments to absorb the impact. In a second sculpture, the scene captures the idea that the protest has had some effect and patrons of the theater have turned away from the screen. Again, allow a few moments to absorb the implications of that scene. Then begin the questions for the debrief: What insights came from the two scenes? What does it take for people to shift from mindless consumption of violence to something more life affirming?

Whether you experiment with planned small group activities or spontaneous large group exchanges, your teaching repertoire can grow and your understanding of learning — and your students — should also deepen. In a world bristling with far too many weapons and much too much violence, where too many think first of military "solutions" to complex problems, where "might makes right," education that empowers through performance can play a special role in defining other alternatives and skills needed to resolve conflicts peacefully.

Chapter 10

STORYTELLING

Stories can be powerfully simple mechanisms to engage audiences and stimulate learning. The rich details of lives, events and places draw us in and speak volumes about underlying beliefs and values. Without analysis or judgment, we are left to come to our own conclusions, much like audiences in the theater. Given the controversies that often surround peace activists, stories can be a powerful ally, for example, as they confront a government's war-making, propaganda machinery and attempt to challenge mindless or misplaced patriotism.

Dorothy Day (1897-1980), co-founder of the Catholic Worker movement was a masterful storyteller. She was also a tireless champion of peace and social justice. Her outlet, St. Joseph's House of Hospitality in New York City, fed hundreds every day. Many received needed medical attention. It produced a monthly paper with 100,000 copies printed and mailed, held public meetings every Friday night, and organized demonstrations for civil rights or peace. The farm associated with this program grew food, canned certain items, and baked bread.

For Dorothy Day, stories drew on traditional church teaching methodologies, encasing particular lessons within descriptions of people and events. A good story about Dorothy herself captures much about her that a conventional biography might miss.

> [In 1962] she addressed a large meeting one night at New York University. As often happened, some of those present found her pacifism naïve and infuriating. One of them demanded to know what she would do if the Russians invaded the United States. Perhaps even she would in that extremity allow that killing was in order. "I would open my heart and my arms and receive them with love, the same as anyone else," she said. It is nearly a biblical quotation. Certainly one is hard pressed to imagine Christ with a machine gun held in his arms, or its equivalent in any age. (Forest 2000, 108)

Even the strongest of psyches can wilt under the weight of the daily responsibilities taken on by the Dorothy Days of this world. Inevitably, challenges to the establishment can take a real emotional toll. It's easy to get caught up in big movements. However, when you take a closer look, you see a lightness, at times an irreverence, that allowed Dorothy and everyone else to enjoy lighter moments within the work, to laugh at each other's idiosyncrasies. A smile comes easily when you read Jim Forest's next story. Notice all his embellishments and word choices.

> One day another member of staff and I were preparing a small apartment into which Dorothy was moving in order to have only one flight of steps to climb instead of five. It was a cold-water slum flat such as ought to have disappeared with Oliver Twist. The place was filled with debris, which we loaded into boxes and carried down to the street. One of the objects we found was a large piece of plywood on which some unknown hand had painted the Holy Family — Mary, Joseph, and Jesus. If there was a style called primitive, this was pre-primitive. After expressing horror with the work's aesthetic poverty, we put it out on the street with the rest of the trash. Soon afterward Dorothy walked in with it, delighted. "Look what I found outside! The Holy Family! It's a providential sign, a blessing." She put it proudly on the mantel of the apartment's extinct fireplace, and it later followed her to other rooms. (2000, 108)

Entire associations have grown up to keep the ancient traditions of storytelling alive. Books have been written and workshops regularly organized for those who want to develop these skills. With practice, teachers at all levels can learn to use their voices more effectively, to add inflection, to adjust their timing, and add pauses for reflection. The simplest gesture can add important emphasis. A simple prop or bit of clothing can enhance an effect. Attention to this level of detail can augment a message, making the embedded "lessons" so much more memorable. (See my 2002 *Teaching and Performing,* co-authored with Burgoyne for more on storytelling.) Like other forms of performance, telling stories brings a personal and human side to lessons and discussions, especially important when we are attempting to de-program those otherwise addicted to violence as a preferred response to conflict.

Chapter 11

MULTI-MODAL DELIVERY
& EXPERIENTIAL LEARNING

Students often struggle to stay focused in traditional classes. Their worlds already overflow with sounds and images, music, and video games, television, movies, cell phones, and computers. Violence sells tickets at the box office. Murder mysteries get our attention because lives hang in the balance. So many previews of adventure movies literally burst with explosions, killings, and terror. The very tone of commercial television has become more intense as advertisers press their fifteen- and thirty-second messages into every possible crack and crevice of consumer consciousness.

These same technologies can be harnessed for learning. In my 1982 book with David Tobin, *Teaching as Performing,* we noted the claims of language instructors who reported on the benefits of adding images and sounds to their teaching, helping students lower their anxiety while helping them focus their minds. Of course, as with other techniques, caution is called for. Using film clips in class, for example, can have a powerful effect, yet violent images may leave an ugly memory trace. You will need to think about whether on not you should shield students from bloody and brutal scenes of historical reenactments.

Direct experience outside the classroom can also affect learning. For example, some people who grow up in privileged communities may not see what connects their life styles to the ever growing demands on the world's finite resources and threats to our shared environment. So often these are major sources of violent conflicts and military responses. You can help counter some of these problems by creating a more student-centered process or by bringing a university course to a developing country. Experiential activities can impact learning and leave indelible memories. Architect and colleague Brian Dunbar located one of his own courses on sustainable building design at a renowned eco-friendly resort on St. John's Maho Bay in the U.S. Virgin Islands. Once there, students were able to see first hand the links between that island's violent past of slavery and European exploitation and the devastating environmental damage that resulted.

This chapter explores the impact on student learning of using a multi-modal style of delivery that contains historically accurate but disturbing images of violence or an experiential context that has itself a grim history. The chapter offers several teaching examples that can raise awareness about violence and deepen learning about constructive alternatives. While some time is lost in the classroom when compared to a more traditional emphasis on lecturing and content coverage, much more seems to have been gained with heightened student engagement, motivation, and understanding.

THE POWER OF FILM

Film clips can augment instruction in engaging and dramatic ways, providing students with powerful images and sounds, and a shared classroom experience that can serve as a reference point for learning, application, analysis, synthesis, and evaluation. Students in my classes often mention my use of short movie excerpts as a course strength. When I debrief other classes around mid-semester as part of my role as Director of the Center for Teaching and Learning at Colorado State University, I get similar kinds of comments — that students appreciate how films can provide concrete and memorable examples of the theories and ideas under study.

Hollywood can pack a lot into a few minutes! However, it is because of that visual and auditory power that some care must be taken to adequately prepare and debrief students. Three examples will illustrate this power and this caution.

BASKETBALL DIARIES

Ever since the 1997 killings at Columbine High School, I have used a clip from the film, *Basketball Diaries* starring Leonardo DeCaprio to illustrate how some individuals, modeling what they see in a movie, will resort to violence as a response to feeling marginalized or persecuted. They will seek revenge, and perhaps notoriety, by gunning down perceived tormentors. The "dream sequence" in this movie, induced by drugs as he soaks in a bathtub and writes in his journal, shows DeCaprio, dressed in a long black leather coat, bursting into a classroom and shooting classmates. How life can imitate art! Although the movie character wakes up and moves on, ultimately getting his life together, the Columbine killers chose to focus on this killing scene, making reference to it in their emails as they planned and then executed their "revenge." While some students, and especially those with direct links to Columbine High School in Colorado, have found this clip deeply disturbing, most see it as directly relevant and useful for illustrating course concepts of "emotional intelligence" and "cognitive development." The question remains, however: Do these scenes add to an existing memory bank of violent images that only serves to desensitize or can they be memorable links to important new insights about peaceful alternatives?

AMISTAD

In a similar way, I have used a clip about the "middle passage" from Spielberg's film, *Amistad,* to add emotional and visual power to discussions about the horrors of slavery. Too often, discussions about the legacy of slavery have seemed superficial, lacking real depth of empathy and understanding. While a few students have said that these scenes were "too brutal" to watch, most have judged them as valuable "reality checks," adding something important to what they were reading, especially meaningful in an age when television, film and media, in general, so dominate what we see. Developmentalists like Bruner (1966) and Piaget (1952) have long argued for attention to the concrete underpinnings of thinking.

GANDHI

At a time in history when violence can take on a horrific life of its own, too often escalating into a death struggle of revenge and retaliation, Gandhi's legacy of nonviolent thought and action remain an enduring foundation for the pursuit of peace. Images of British ordered brutality toward unarmed Indian people are juxtaposed throughout the film with Gandhi's own repeated commitment to the moral high ground of nonviolent non-cooperation. These visual and auditory memories seem to last, much more than what is only seen in print. As such they can compete with what we all saw on television when those hijacked airliners hit New York's World Trade Center.

THE POWER OF EXPERIENTIAL LEARNING

In a similar way, field-based learning can add powerful, real world experiences to course content, energizing learning, deepening understanding, addressing underlying values and, at times, contributing to creative, new possibilities. In two different classes on sustainable architecture and construction, Brian Dunbar drew on David Orr's (1994) powerful commentaries about the "pedagogy of architecture" and involved students in simulations of design practices. In each case, issues were made more real and learning was deepened. As a scholar of post-secondary instruction, I participated in each class, contributing some content but mostly observing the teaching process and noting its impact on learning.

COLLABORATIVE DESIGNS

For a campus course on sustainable design, Dunbar took on an actual building project at Colorado State University as the focus for small group design collaboration. The resulting activities were varied and complex, impacted by the communication skills of the students as well as by their learning styles, backgrounds, and motivations. Opportunities to visit the nearby proposed building site allowed for a student-centered process which seemed to blend the "space" necessary for creativity, both literally and figuratively, with the reality of a particular piece of land. In addition, we realized that we needed time together and a climate of mutual respect to challenge established paradigms and imagine new possibilities. When the

Department Head and two of his key faculty members arrived for the presentation on the last day, they saw — and felt — our collective enthusiasm, creativity, and commitment for sustainable design and construction. By allowing the time for exploration and input, deeply held values about environmentally sustainable practices could be shared and addressed.

Maho Bay

Employing similar student-centered practices, Dunbar also recruited a group of students to join him in the U.S. Virgin Islands on St. John to study sustainable design and construction at a resort which itself was internationally famous for following principles of ecological design. Unlike high-end resorts nearby — air conditioners buzzing in solar-oblivious buildings over large, manicured lawns where the local sources of drinking water have all been spoiled — the Maho Bay eco-resort blends tent structures and connecting boardwalks into the forested landscape. Students meet and work in open air pavilions that model a much lighter, more respectful relationship to the land. Yet, despite absolutely stunning sunsets, students were also challenged to consider the terrible ecological toll that early European colonizers had exacted, clear cutting the island and expropriating slave labor to make sugar cane production possible and lucrative. Dunbar's use of meditations and music added even more power to the depth of this learning experience.

Final course assessments from students give testimony to the effectiveness of a field-based, multi-modal experience:

- "A positive life-changing, thought-provoking, and inspirational twelve days of learning."

- "The material of the course, the manner in which it was presented, and the place have had a significant impact on my life."

- "Having the class material presented at a place like Maho Bay is like seeing yourself in the mirror for the first time."

- "Without a doubt, this was the greatest academic experience in my life. The location of the course naturally leads to reflection and personal learning."

COGNITIVE DEVELOPMENT
AND LEARNING STYLES

One way to understand the impact reflected in these course assessments is to look at the literature on cognitive development and learning styles. Knowing students more as individuals and knowing the stages they move through can go far in guiding instructors through the complexities associated with multi-modal and experiential approaches (see Armstrong, 1995; Bruner, 1966; Deese & Deese, 1994; Gardner & Jewler, 1997; Longman & Atkinson, 1999; Perry, 1999; Piaget, 1952; Timpson, 1999; Walter & Siebert, 1996). Much in life is about learning and adaptation. The challenge, however, becomes this: How can instruction be both engaging and efficient? How quickly can students adjust to new and different demands, overcoming their own limitations, prejudices, and predispositions? When events explode upon us, our ability to think beyond old paradigms and consider creative alternatives can make all the difference. As instructors, we can help students understand the various ways they can think about their own development, learning styles, and preferences, about what works best and why. We can use film, music, and/or field experience to build on their strengths as well as address areas of weaknesses. These different modes of teaching can be very effective in reaching students who vary widely in the way they learn.

FOR ACTIVE TO PASSIVE LEARNERS

Many students need to be active to learn best. Developmental psychologists like Jean Piaget (1952) and Jerome Bruner (1966) have long noted the importance of the various senses in learning, and recognized how physical manipulation can be an essential foundation for understanding concepts, theories, and other abstractions. Yet, college instructors often neglect the need for active student learning, especially when large classes make alternatives to lecturing problematic. For students new to campus, a more passive role usually means a huge adjustment given the more intimate, interactive settings they were used to in high school. Admittedly, some students will say they like the anonymity of big college classes; they can hide out with impunity. Films, music, and experiential learning, however, tend to engage everyone, no matter where they may fall on the continuum from active to passive. Here are some ideas for making the most of these kinds of alternative learning environments.

- Emphasize journaling and good note taking. Students can be active in writing out what they hear, see, and feel. While there can never be any "correct" response to a particular movie scene, written reactions can foster self-reflection, lead toward new insights, and mitigate against the imprinting of unprocessed violent images. Descriptive journaling and self-discovery were linked with and by the film clips I used as well as with and by Dunbar's cooperative design project and field-based course at Maho Bay.

- Suggest that students add questions in the margins of their class notes. What's confusing? What implications do they see? How does the film, music, or field experience connect to what they've been hearing in class? They can have a running conversation with their instructors inside their own heads. These will make for great starter topics both inside and outside class.

- Suggest that students form a study group early in a semester. Explaining what they think to others and hearing what others have to say can help them clarify their own thinking.

- Suggest that students move closer to the front of class. This recommendation helps many students. However, especially in a large lecture hall, films and music typically play well to big audiences, better engaging even the back rows of even reluctant learners.

FOR REFLECTIVE TO IMPULSIVE LEARNERS

Jerome Bruner (1966) has also reported that knowing student preferences for reflection or more impulsive action can be very useful for instructors. For example, you yourself may be the type of person who needs time and space to think through what you hear. When students feel that they are supposed to make an immediate response to an instructor's questions in class, some may feel anxious and/or intimidated. On the other hand, learning to speak up and participate actively in discussions can prove enormously valuable, and not just in school. For example, can you think of any work environment where you are totally alone all of the time? Even writers who need absolute isolation to concentrate fully have to meet with publishers and readers periodically. Artists may have to communicate with potential buyers. Performers always work in collaboration with a crew of some kind and often meet with audience members or reviewers.

Responding to films, music, and field experiences can help impulsive learners begin to reflect on their emotional reactions. Those who are more reflective can learn to assess their more immediate responses. While the peace movement has historically called on a whole range of talents, protests and demonstrations do require a certain willingness to be seen and heard in public. For students who are more reflective, you might try these techniques:

- Encourage them to participate actively in class, while using the quiet of the library or their own rooms to reflect, clarify, organize and prepare. Providing lecture notes can relieve some of the pressure on them to get "every word down."

- Provide some time for students to meet in small groups to talk over your questions or assignments with one or two others before a general class discussion begins. You may have some students who seem to learn best by speaking up, who clarify their own thinking through talking. In a large class this can be a problem but one you can satisfy, in part, with regular small group interactions.

- If a few students are dominating class discussions and you want to get others involved, ask for responses from "those who have not participated" or encourage the use of office hours or email for discussions outside of class.

- Have students make presentations in class about topics of their choosing. Tapping into their interests as well as providing opportunities for students to prepare outside of class will allow quieter students to participate more.

- Allow time in class for students to reflect and meditate. As happens in Quaker meetings, these periods of quiet can be a source of important personal insights.

- Study groups can be a wonderful mechanism for impulsive students to take proactive responsibility for their own learning styles. Note that the more you can help them understand their own preferences, the better able they will be to learn with others, to communicate what works for them, and to ask for what they need in order to be better learners. If they learn these skills, they will be more prepared to understand the levels of complexity introduced by films, music, and field experiences.

- You can also help impulsive students develop their reflective abilities by using their class notes to write out (and think about) their questions.

FOR AUDITORY, VISUAL, AND KINESTHETIC LEARNERS

You probably have some sense of how you yourself learn best, if it is through sight, sound, touch, or some combination of all three (Sarasin, 1998). Doing well in school or college often requires students to adapt, to use their strengths, and compensate for their weaknesses as well as develop new skills. For example, if your students learn best visually, you might find that their attention wanders during presentations. They may miss important points when they can't "see" — literally and figuratively — the concepts and interrelationships in some kind of chart or diagram. If they learn best through hearing, they may find themselves thrown off by lectures dominated by slides or PowerPoint presentations. If they do best with hands-on learning, they may struggle in big lecture classes without some kind of lab or field experience where they can participate in more practical applications. Films allow multi-modal engagement, and so are effective in getting the attention of a broad range of students. Consider the possibility that you can be more effective teaching something about peace if you can use relevant film clips.

Here are some techniques for helping students use their auditory, visual, or kinesthetic skills.

- Encourage them to analyze their own strengths and weaknesses, then share ideas for improvement. For example, if they are visual, they could concentrate on creating "conceptual maps" or drawings that diagram and connect major points in the readings or lecture with what was depicted in a film or what arose in the field.

- Encourage students to get together with classmates whose strengths complement their own. For instance, they could identify others whose notes are more complete and better organized than their own or whose reactions to the music were different. Polling a class about their learning styles and preferences might help students find those who have complementary styles.

FOR CONCRETE TO ABSTRACT LEARNERS

Anthony Gregorc (1982) has articulated a system which many instructors and students find useful for the continuum of learners whose preference runs from the *concrete* to the *abstract*. Some students seem to need a real grounding in the details of any subject before they can move to what is more abstract and theoretical. Other students seem to thrive on ideas. They live in their heads, as it were. Here are some suggestions to help you lay groundwork for using films and field experiences as concrete reference points for analysis and critical thinking.

- If students are more concrete learners, if they need to get involved with the material, you can provide more examples that illustrate key concepts. Ask your students if they need more hands on experiences. Ask them for additional examples that make sense to them.

- If students are more abstract learners and love ideas, you can ask them about underlying concepts. You can create *concept maps* that organize the course material according to a hierarchy of categories, super-categories and sub-categories. Think about the complexity of issues surrounding the violence in the Middle East or Northern Ireland, for example, or what has been our own continuing response to the threat of terrorist attacks. A concept map can provide a useful visual and organizing reference.

FOR SEQUENTIAL TO RANDOM LEARNERS

For Gregorc, another useful distinction is whether learners tend to move in a very sequential fashion or prefer to skip about in whatever direction seems most promising. Note that this distinction looks similar to what Bruner (1966) reported as the reflective/impulsive continuum. In groups, the *sequential* people tend to be very organized. It can be difficult for them to accommodate those who are more *random* in their thinking, who have less need for planning, and seem to thrive on the energy of a more creative process. Invariably, groups that work well together have both types, as well as others who are at different places between these two extremes.

- In class, if you have students who are more sequential in their thinking, you may find that some of them become frustrated with questions which seem to take a lecture off onto tangents, or when films and field-based experiences require complex responses. You can help them understand the source of their frustration and how it can serve as a catalyst for learning.

- If you have students who are more random in their thinking, they may become bored with a highly organized and linear lecture. Creating concept maps of the material or new acronyms to assist memorization can be fun and engaging. Using movie clips, music, or field experiences can add some welcome stimulation for these kinds of students.

FOR QUIET TO NOISY LEARNERS

Some students need quiet to concentrate while others seem to function better with music in the background. Some prefer to study alone while others learn best in interactive group situations. Some people want to focus on one task at a time while others are good at multi-tasking. What is your own ability to handle noise and concentrate on complex assignments? What works where and for which subjects? How can you best help students to navigate these factors? Providing rich, multi-modal environments for learning also serves as a useful assessment strategy to help you see what works best for which students.

- You can encourage students to experiment with different conditions to see what works best for them. You can demonstrate this in class by assigning a task and, then, varying the conditions (noise, light, temperature, space) while asking students to reflect on their preferences.

• You can also help them notice what others do, where, and when. Many students will make good use of the library as a place to go for quiet. Others will stake out places on campus or a local coffee house.

CONCLUSIONS ON THE VALUE OF MULTI-MODAL DELIVERY

While there may be some risks to instructor control and content coverage when film, music, and experiential learning are employed, the impact on students can be profound. Many will value examples from movies and the field because important course concepts are illustrated in a mode that is impactful and familiar. As mentioned, developmentalists like Piaget (1952) and Bruner (1966) have long championed concrete "hands-on" experiences as a necessary foundation for building solid abstractions. Otherwise, students fall back on attempting to memorize what they hope will be on a test, cramming responses into short-term memory, and just as quickly forgetting much of what went in.

Assessments of Dunbar's and my own courses indicate that our use of film, music, and field experiences seems to have deepened student learning, extending course impact far beyond the curriculum while raising awareness about fundamental values and beliefs. Our own appreciation of the importance of multi-modal delivery has grown accordingly. While these kinds of alternatives to traditional course delivery take some time to design and organize, the benefits seem well worth the effort. Indeed, the student excitement that resulted in our courses has had a positive impact on our own motivations. It has also created some tangible synergy where the benefits to individuals combined to enhance the total course experience for everyone. These benefits seem especially important to us at a time when the enormity of various forces and events — terrorist attacks and military responses, income inequities and cries for social justice, enduring racism and sexism, historical and religious conflicts, environmental degradation, and human responsibilities — can overwhelm more traditional dispassionate intellectual analyses so typical of academic learning.

For the purpose of teaching and learning peace, multi-modal delivery and experiential learning can help us raise awareness about the all too pervasive nature of violence spread throughout American culture and aggressively exported worldwide through film, television and gangster rap music. In a provocative essay, *Saying No to Death,* Dutch-born priest and writer Henri Nouwen decries the violence laced into a supposed comedy like the film, *The Blues Brothers.*

> What does it mean when young, ambitious Americans are being entertained with millions of dollars worth of destruction in a world where many people die from fear, lack of food, and ever-increasing violence?...Once I met a Vietnam veteran in an airplane. He told me that he had seen so many people killed on television that it had been hard for him to believe that those whom *he* killed would not stand up again to act in the next movie. Death had become unreal. Vietnam had woke him up to the truth that death is real and final and very ugly. When I am honest with myself, I have to confess that I, too, am often seduced by the titillating power of death. I look with open eyes and open mouth as stunt pilots, motorcyclists, and car racers put their lives at risk in their desire to break a record or perform a dizzying feat. In this respect I am little different from the thousands of Romans who were entertained by the life-and-death game of the gladiators, or from the crowds who in the past and even the present are attracted to places of public execution. (2000, 143-144)

Raising awareness on these issues is of key importance, especially when the way in which we raise awareness — our mode of delivery — helps students recognize the connection between large issues and their own lives. The Nobel Peace Laureate, Vietnamese Buddhist monk Thich Nhat Hanh, has written extensively about the importance of being aware of the links between the simplest actions in our daily lives and the compelling bigger issues.

> I think the most important precept of all is to live in awareness, to know what is going on — not only here but there. For instance, when we eat a piece of bread, we may choose to be aware of how our farmers grow the wheat. It seems that chem-

ical poisons are used a bit too much. And while we eat the bread, we are somehow co-responsible for the destruction of our ecology. When we eat a piece of meat, we may become aware that eating meat is not a good way to reconcile oneself with millions of children in the world. Forty thousand children die each day in the Third World for lack of food. And in order to produce meat, you have to feed the cow or the chicken with a lot of cereal…What we are, what we do every day, has much to do with world peace. If we are aware of our lifestyle, our way of consuming and looking at things, then we know how to make peace right at the present moment. If we are very aware, we will do something to change the course of things. (2000, 156)

Chapter 12

Exercises & Activities

Drawing on Experience, Feelings, and Intuitions

Over the years I have tried a number of different exercises and activities in my explorations of teaching and learning. Two of my earlier books, *Concepts and Choices for Teaching* (1996) and *Teaching and Performing* (2002) have questions and/or exercises at the end of each chapter. The activities, exercises, and questions that follow reinforce the explorations and classroom applications covered in both Parts I and II of this book. They do so through exercises that help us draw on experience as well as on feelings and intuitions. You will recognize the connections to earlier chapters.

Meditations

My colleague, Nat Kees, a counselor by training, brought some wonderful ideas for centering to our class on *Teaching and Learning Peace*. Drawing on the practices of Thich Nhat Hanh, for example, she offered organically grown grapes to everyone and asked us to focus before we ate, to reflect on the "vastness" that was imbedded in each grape. She asked us to think about the earth, sun, and rain that nurtured its growth, the farmer's commitment to be gentle on the land and limit the use of chemical fertilizers and pesticides, the hands that picked and packaged it, those who drove it to our community, placed it on the shelves. She asked us to look at our grape closely, its color and shape. Mindfulness was the point. Nat, then had us put the grape in our mouths and roll it around for a bit, feeling its shape as it began to mix with our own saliva. We then savored that very first bite, aware of new taste sensations from this slower, more mindful process.

On subsequent mornings of our workshop on *Teaching and Learning Peace*, we explored other possibilities for mindfulness. Nat loaned me a large poster of the New York City skyline taken before September 11, 2001. We breathed in the suffering of those lost in the World Trade Center, we breathed out the possibilities for lessons learned and a rebirth for the city. I had a framed photograph of a Native American chief next to the poster. We breathed in the years of suffering in the wake of the arrival of Europeans and breathed out possibilities for rediscovering old indigenous truths about living in harmony with the land. We remembered the scene from Spike Lee's film on Malcolm X where a pilgrimage to Mecca prompted a conversion. We "breathed in" the years of brutal oppression and systemic prejudice visited upon Africans brought to the United States as slaves and "breathed out" the gifts we all enjoy from our African American brothers and sisters.

On the last morning, I used a small set of hand cymbals I had gotten outside a temple in Katmandu, Nepal the previous summer. The clear resonating tones helped to evoke yet another morning meditation. In class we had commented on the difficulty we all had separating our memories of past horrors from a need to forgive, heal, and move on. We all struggled with the seeming intransigence of violence in the Middle East between Israelis and Palestinians. We worried about the emphasis on retaliation against terrorists "everywhere" in post-9/11 America. One of our class members had been involved with restorative work in Rwanda after the genocidal killings. On this particular morning, I asked for a merging, remembering, and forgiveness in a way that honors the past but allows us to move forward toward an inclusive, just and fair future. I rang the cymbals after each appeal.

For healing . . .

For moving past revenge . . .

For remembering and forgiving . . .

For the reconciliation leadership of Nelson Mandela and Bishop Tutu . . .

For healing the wounds of slavery and the legacy of racism . . .

For what we can learn from Native Americans about the land . . .

For all immigrant groups who came for a better life . . .

For addressing poverty and the unfairness of great wealth . . .

For moving punishment into learning . . .

For deeper listening, more empathy and consensus . . .

For reducing waste . . .

For conserving energy . . .

For reusing goods and materials . . .

For restoring the health of the air, water and land . . .

For being in harmony with all living entities . . .

For living more gently on the earth . . .

MUSIC

Sounds can also lead us to explore meaning at a different level, finding core truths in the midst of the complexities that comprise peacemaking. For one of our introductory meditations, we listened to a hauntingly simple bamboo flute from Nepal. On another day we heard sacred drumming by a Native American group. As a lead-in to an exercise on hopefulness, I played a song by Sweet Honey and the Rock, an acappella group of African American women whose repertoire addresses issues of social justice, faith, and struggle. In *"I Remember, I Believe"* they marvel at their people's resilience despite years of suffering. This is the song that I played on September 11 in my large lecture class just after we heard about the attacks and while those televised images were still so raw and disturbing.

> I don't know how my mother walked her trouble down
> I don't know how my father stood his ground
> I don't know how my people survived slavery
> I do remember, that's why I believe

During the week in *Teaching and Learning Peace*, we also listened to a version of the *National Anthem* that a class member brought in. We heard a rendition of *Down by the Riverside* by the Blind Boys of Alabama and their determined, "I ain't gonna study war no more...." Jimmy Cliff's reggae versions of *The Harder They Come* and *Johnny Too Bad* gave us testimonials to the dangers of poverty and violence, while Bob Marley's *One World* reminded us of the love that was possible despite the most oppressive of conditions. Zap Mama added a wonderful upbeat and international flavor. Later, when we took some time to debrief what was working in class, everyone seemed to value this attention to multiple modalities as well as the rich legacy of song in movements for peace and social justice.

MOVIES AND VIDEOS

Film clips gave us another shared experience to hold and remember. *Stand and Deliver* tells Jaime Escalante's remarkable story of coming from Bolivia to teach mathematics at Garfield High School in the East Los Angeles barrio and helping students exceed everyone's expectations. In our meditation, we breathed in the scenes of fighting and breathed out our belief in their ability to find alternatives to conflict resolution. We breathed in the poverty of the area and breathed out our knowledge that some could really succeed with what Escalante termed *"ganas,"* desire. We breathed in the apathy of the teaching staff and breathed out the power in Jaime's high expectations for students and himself. He was always ready to admit that he "could do more." We breathed in the gang members and their dislike for school and breathed out the creative courage some showed in breaking free to feed their minds. We breathed in Escalante's confrontational teasing and breathed out his ability to energize his connection with even the toughest students.

I also showed a videotape of the Discovery Program and its founder, alternative high school teacher Eric Larsen who lives in Ft. Collins, Colorado and works in the Poudre Schools. Eric's work has evolved from twenty-five years with at-risk kids — gang members and "wanna be's," survivors of family abuse and neglect, too susceptible to the influences of drinking and drugs, too quick to fight, and largely unskilled in alternatives to anger and violence. Without the benefits of federal or corporate support, but with the backing of a generous friend, Larsen has created a skill-based focus that is effective at all grade levels and has now been adopted in fifteen states. This videotape provides direct testimony from teachers, counselors, administrators, and students in some very tough schools that a focus on anger management and life skills can provide the kind of foundation for success too often neglected in our current national preoccupation with academic achievement and testing.

Food and restaurants

Along with linking simple foods, mindfulness, and increased awareness in our meditations — the organic grape, for example, that Nat Kees used to remind us of the role of sunshine and rain, the farmers and drivers — others in the class also brought contributions of food to share. Mango slices on one day. A large bag of animal cookies on another. These were especially appreciated given the length of this three hour class. On the last morning we broke bread from two fresh baguettes and again practiced a mindful meditation with strawberries from California and grapes from Mexico. We worried about the potential violence to the land from buying non-organic fruits, as well as the implications for fossil fuel use and pollution from transporting foods such long distances.

During the week, one of our class members also sampled foods at local ethnic restaurants, using the opportunity to talk about peace from a cross cultural perspective. At the nearby Indian restaurant she got to ask about the tensions with Pakistan about Kashmir. At a Middle Eastern restaurant, she had a wonderful conversation with the chef and waitress about immigration and the fears among Muslims after September 11. At a Mexican restaurant, she could ask about the legacy of racism in our own community given its historic dependence on migrant and Hispanic laborers.

Peace mandalas

After class, our fourth grade teacher worked with an eleven year old to create and color peace mandalas, circles of shapes and swirls of vibrant colors. This kind of artistic creativity can allow teachers and students to meditate on peace in an active, fun and revealing way. Because such a process is itself peaceful, insights can come at any moment. This teacher then told us about being in San Francisco when an angry "deranged" street person burst into the room where four monks were creating a sand mandala and kicked her way through it. Despite the anguish of those who witnessed this attack, the monks themselves were very accepting of what happened, concerned more about the well being of the attacker. They knew from the beginning that they were going to sweep away the mandala at its completion. Its impermanence, like life itself, was the central lesson.

CIRCLE TIME

As part of his Discovery Program, Eric Larsen has found a powerful "check in" mechanism for helping young people experience and practice emotional honesty, acceptance, support, and appreciation for each other. Forty minutes of every day is spent in "circle" where students "check in" with their feelings, using a number from one ("I'm feeling terrible!") to ten ("Life is great today!") as a reference and then a response to the "prompt" for the day (e.g., "What was most valuable from yesterday and why?"). The others in the group are there to listen and empathize, to provide support and assistance. As each person finishes, everyone applauds.

While your classes may be larger — Eric typically has twenty or so students in attendance — and you may not be able to devote this much time for a "circle check in" in your own classes, there are features you could adapt to any small group activity. For example, a few minutes can be given over for group members to check in with each other ("How's everybody doing? Anything big going on?"), offer progress reports, practice good listening skills (using reflections, empathy, summary statements), and celebrate each other's contributions. Peacemaking can happen in incremental ways by practicing good group skills. No matter the size of your class, a check-in can be very valuable for encouraging mutual acceptance and emotional honesty. Something important always seems to happen during these activities, something that is essential if young people are to repair the damage to their psyches and learn some real skills for successfully navigating the world. You can almost see the rationale for Maslow's (1959) hierarchy of needs as students find the safety, acceptance, and sense of belonging they need to learn, risk, and grow.

GRADING

One issue that emerged in our class was the way in which grading might limit or enhance classroom efforts at peacemaking. Grading on a curve, for example, demands a certain number of "winners" and "losers" *by definition* as the top eighteen percent get the As and Bs while the bottom eighteen percent are assigned Ds and Fs. Competition is linked directly to this kind of assessment. While motivating for some, the resulting grades say little about learning in any absolute sense. Given the limited number of high grades that are possible here, it is not surprising that students are reluctant to help each other.

In contrast, a *mastery approach* focuses on established criteria, carefully sequenced instruction and frequent feedback to support student success (e.g., Bloom, 1973). Cooperation is encouraged since good grades are not limited to a certain percentage. As Bloom often argued, with *time, the appropriate materials and instruction, nearly every learner can be successful.* To the extent that conflict often arises out of competition while peacemaking builds upon cooperation, your choice of grading systems will speak volumes about your underlying values.

Reflection papers

In contrast to a more conventional focus on testing what students can recall, assigning reflection papers allows students to reflect on the readings, react to class discussions and activities, find what is most meaningful and comment from a personal standpoint. For example, one class member in our *Teaching and Learning Peace* workshop brought her lived experience overseas to a reading on the Philippino revolution. In that essay, Hildegard Goss-Mayr (2000) described her involvement in helping the church develop nonviolent training in response to the predictable repression of then dictator, Ferdinand Marcos. One of the enduring lessons for peacemaking is the complexity inherent in most issues and the central truth of humility. Despite this writer's conviction that the "United States gave its support to the new government at the very last moment" (p. 253), our student knew that U.S. government officials were working actively behind the scenes to get Marcos to resign and cede power to the opposition headed by Cory Aquino. As teachers and writers, parents and colleagues, we can always remind ourselves of the humility we need, admitting what we don't know and alerting students to what we *think* happened based on the best available information, but staying open to new information and interpretation.

The Classroom Meeting Model
and Mid-Semester Student Feedback

As with the "circle check in," much about peaceful practice, democratic participation and constructive conflict resolution can happen in a classroom meeting or mid-semester student feedback session. Drawing on the work of William Glasser (1969, 1975, 1986, 1992), a clinical psychologist with a long-standing interest in teaching and learning, I can recommend the classroom meeting model for addressing problems that arise or for soliciting feedback from students early enough in a semester so that there is time to make reasonable adjustments. The process involved in this model is designed to be constructive, to promote self-reflection and personal responsibility as students join with instructors in exploring problems and possible improvements.

When the focus of instruction shifts from the *act of teaching* (delivery) to the *process of learning* (what is internal to the student), increasing communication between instructors and students becomes essential. Whether you run the meeting yourself or have someone else facilitate it, holding a classroom meeting to solicit feedback is one proven and constructive way to stop and take stock of a course from the student's perspective. Because you ask for this feedback, because you have a genuine interest in making improvements in the course now and in the future, students are usually very appreciative. They rarely have been included this way. Moreover, they often come up with good ideas that you might have missed if you hadn't asked. Indeed, this process also gets students thinking more about their own learning, their successes and their struggles, their needs, and how best to articulate what they are thinking.

When you run a classroom meeting, you should have certain goals in mind. Remember, however, that feelings — yours and theirs — are important. It's not about right or wrong but what benefits learning or detracts from it. Ensuring that everyone has a chance to be heard helps keep the process real and responsible.

Appreciations

Along with hearing about student concerns you also want to know what is working for them, what you can continue to emphasize and build upon, the positive reinforcement you yourself need. All too often, taking stock of a course gets associated with a "group gripe" session. Without attention to appreciations and recommendations, you run the risk of letting the classroom meeting devolve into a negative process with little that is constructive. In any group, "nay sayers" can dominate and set an overly critical climate. Part of the process I recommend is to ask for what your students appreciate about your class. Remember to express you own appreciations as well, what you enjoy about the students and the content. Addressing concerns and resolving conflicts proceed best from an established base of positive regard.

Empowerment

At core, the classroom meeting model is about student *empowerment;* it's not just a theoretical construct. You are entering a collaborative process with students to consider improvements in a particular course. With this kind of involvement, you can also expect greater ownership from students and an increased willingness to accept course requirements. It is not surprising when students are critical and cynical about classes that never allow any open discussion about improvements. Why should students take seriously the request for thoughtful course evaluations at the end of a semester when any benefits possible are only for future generations? Peacemaking skills build from a source of strength and confidence.

Turning concerns into recommendations

Once you have identified some of the positives about the course, you can safely turn to *perceived* concerns. Here, it is helpful if you insist on *personal responsibility;* students should express their concerns in the first person, with "I" statements about what they think and feel as individuals. Too many people generalize too quickly beyond their own felt experiences; for example, they could say, "This class has too much required reading" as opposed to the more honest "*I feel* that this class has too much required reading." This may seem to be a subtle distinction but it can make a difference in how this message is delivered and received.

In addition, I have also found it important to insist that students link their concerns with recommendations for improvement. For example, as a follow-on to a concern about "too much theory," a student might say, "Because I find my mind wandering in class, I would appreciate more variety, more discussions, perhaps summaries on the overhead projector to help me stay focused on key points, more guest speakers who can share alternative views, more opportunities to work actively in small groups, *stuff like that!*" Again, it is important for you to take a few minutes to voice your own experiences, your frustrations; but, like the students, follow these expressions with your own recommendations for students to consider.

Putting problem solving into action

One important dynamic of the classroom meeting model is the responsibility on your part to take action on those ideas that you believe have merit. If you use the model's process only to air grievances, as some kind of *cathartic group activity,* then you run the risk of doing more damage than good. You will have enticed students into a process where you have no intention of following through. Glasser puts emphasis on the "real." To avoid being put on the spot to make a change on too short a notice — such as changing the course text mid-semester — you can always clarify at the beginning what you are able to change now as opposed to what you will consider for future classes. By and large, students are very accepting of this and appreciative of your interest in hearing their ideas.

The classroom meeting model can also be used for general discussions. It can help ensure widespread participation, personal responsibility, and an ongoing concern for what is "real." It asks everyone to take stock in some issue, to identify personal beliefs based on felt experiences or values or beliefs, and to stay focused on what's practical and achievable.

Shared responsibility

Essential to Glasser's model for a classroom meeting is the idea of shared responsibility, that you and your students take seriously your co-creative roles in exploring course improvements. In fact, given the choice of running the classroom meeting yourself or using a facilitator, Glasser would recommend the former because it adds a measure of personal responsibility when you have to talk with students face-to-face. It's less likely that you will get any "cheap shots." It can be important for you to hear directly from students about their likes and dislikes; and they need to hear form you. Peacemaking is always a shared journey.

Rejecting the irresponsible

Along with a commitment to this process of shared responsibility, Glasser also calls for a rejection of the "irresponsible," those ideas that are not reasonable or possible. For example, I have heard some students advocate for a dramatic lessening of requirements ("Lets do away with the exams." Or, "Get rid of some of the required reading."). Here, it can be very helpful to have a frank discussion of what are appropriate expectations for a course created at a particular level ("No, we cannot eliminate all graded assignments." Or, "A university course at this level typically has certain kinds of expectations, readings, etc."). Asking students to compare your course expectations with what they have experienced in other departments can also prove useful. Peacemaking is built on with honest and direct communication.

Full and public participation

Another process piece of Glasser's model is the requirement for full and public participation. As I have used this model, students shift from completing individual responses to small group discussions to a large group forum on particular issues. This kind of process allows individuals to express their opinions in a private and protected manner while participating simultaneously in a more public assessment. When peace movements succeed, they also tend to have widespread and active involvement.

Facilitator skills

To make the best use of the classroom meeting model, the session leader — whether you do it yourself or invite someone else in — should have in hand certain skills mentioned in Part I. *Listening* should be reflective and deep. Students may be asked to clarify their comments. *Empathy* can also be important as a way to encourage students to go further in their thinking; for example, saying "It seems that the lack of clarity would be frustrating" might permit a student to go deeper to identify more concretely the problem and its importance. *Acceptance* is another process skill that can open doors to deeper and more honest dialogue, especially if you run the session yourself. You may disagree with a comment, but it is very important that you acknowledge a student's felt experience. Finally, *consensus* is a useful goal for both the small and large group components, especially when you want to negotiate concrete improvements. Skilled mediation can stop conflicts and help those involved find mutually acceptable and constructive ways forward.

THE INSTRUCTIONAL MAP

Providing what I refer to as an Instructional Map for the classroom meeting (Timpson, 1999) can give you a visual overview of the goals and procedures for the meeting. In the sample below, note that the vertical axis represents a continuum which moves from attention to *product* (information, facts, skills, dealing with the concrete) to *process* (thinking, working with abstractions, creating, communicating, cooperating). The horizontal axis represents your choices for instruction, from teacher-directed (e.g., lecture, demonstration, programmed instruction) to student-centered (e.g., discussion, discovery, questions, and answers, review sessions). The third dimension lets you move from large to small group experiences to individual assignments. Peacemaking requires a certain degree of sophistication given the typically complex mix of values, behaviors and emotions at play when conflicts erupt. The Instructional Map provides a useful degree of distance as you keep in perspective the more important factors in learning.

A LAST WORD ON THE ELEMENTS OF THE CLASSROOM MEETING

Like the town meeting, the classroom meeting is a mechanism for soliciting formative feedback and problem solving. Everyone, including the teacher, is encouraged to express thoughts and feelings about the class, instruction, and learning, both in writing and orally in public. Appreciations are reinforcing; they strengthen what works. The focus on individual responsibility means that concerns are linked to recommendations. Taking action on reasonable and achievable recommendations helps put meaning to the process.

#1. Create climate of involvement

#2. Define problem

#3. Make personal value judgment

#4. Identify alternatives

#5. Make a commitment

#6. Follow up

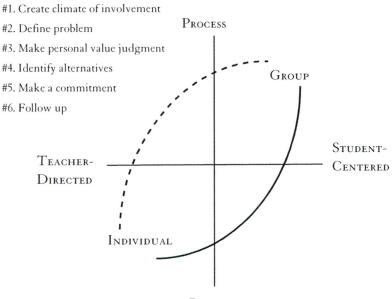

Instructional Map

Mid-Semester Student Feedback
CLASSROOM MEETING

Adapted from Timpson & Bendel-Simso (1997)

Conclusion:
A Culture of Peace

Knowledge and understanding are at the heart of the educational mission and just as essential for peacemaking. We have to know when humans have been able to turn away from violence and avoid war, when the powerful have been willing to share control with those on the margins, when a commitment to social justice, economic fairness, and environmental responsibility can address the underlying tensions that often spark conflicts in other cultures.

However, we also have to recognize how challenging the study of peace really is. Wars can be traced to their origins and various explanations offered based on the historical record. A study of peace, in turn, has much less certainty to it. Just how do we give credit, to whom, and how much? Explanations vie for attention. Yes, a cease fire can be ordered just as an attack can be started. Maintaining the peace in times of tension, for example, or finding ways to resolve conflicts without resorting to violence inevitably requires a mix of factors and the commitment of many to achieve.

Elise Boulding, a sociologist by training, is one of our best known scholars on peace. In *Cultures of Peace,* she offers a compelling overview of the road we've taken, in all its troubling complexities, as well as the direction we need to go.

> In general, societies tend to be a blend of peaceable and warrior culture themes — the balance between the themes varying from society to society and from historical moment to historical moment. In our time, the tensions between the two themes have become a heavy social burden as a worldwide military forcing system linked to a destructive, planet-harming mode of industrialization and urbanization is distorting the human capability for creative and peaceful change. No sooner did the fears of nuclear holocaust fade with the end of the Cold War then the fear of genocidal ethnic warfare, reducing once proudly independent countries to a series of dusty battlegrounds, rose to take the place of earlier fears. Urban violence — now manifesting itself in gun battles in the cities and neighborhoods and even the schoolyards and playgrounds of the industrial West — has unleashed other terrors. If every society is a blend of the themes of violence and peaceableness, why is the peaceableness so hard to see? It is there, but not well reported. The tendency of planners and policymakers to prepare for worst-case scenarios leaves societies unprepared for the opportunities involved in best-case scenarios. (2000, 4)

The connection for me between teaching, learning, and peacemaking lies, in part, with a mixing of principles from the mastery model, where success (peace) is a central focus with cooperative, experiential learning, critical and creative thinking. Both the *art* and *science* of instruction are, then, applied to create opportunities to practice lessons learned. At a skill level, the curriculum is sequenced in small enough steps to ensure learning (mastery). Knowledge, understanding, skill, and some *wisdom* (i.e., intelligence, critical analysis) are then joined in real world applications whenever possible. In her final chapter, Boulding goes on to frame the future of hope as a function of the learning that is needed.

> We are in the middle of rough times as I write, and much rougher times lie ahead. The challenge is to draw on the best of

the hopes and the best of the learning skills, and the relationship-building networking, and coalition-forming skills that have developed in this past century, so that the long-term future may yet birth new cultures of peace. (2000, 257)

On a very personal level, my eleven year old daughter, Jayme, epitomizes the potential for this culture of peace. Despite a rough six months in an Oakland school, a minority herself for the first time, she could still make friends and see signs of progress as she wrote: "Remember that in the hard times there is hope. There will be a future." After moving to Santa Cruz, she later came back to San Francisco to participate in the March 20, 2002 peace march and found renewed support for her own youthful hopefulness — and her hope for the future is the best place to leave this extended discussion of teaching and learning peace.

> When I reached the top of one hill, I looked back. My breath was taken away. Two hundred yards of activists with banners, flags, music and placards all marching for peace. In Washington, D.C. they had 40,000 marchers. Here in San Francisco, we had 15,000. It blew me away how many cops there were. One at every corner and one in between. It was a bit scary because a few people got arrested. It was almost like the cops wanted to bust the crowd and put some people in jail. In the march I dressed in green, a color for solidarity, and held an earth flag. The actual march was about a mile and a half. We walked by a moving sound system with a ground shaking beat that kept us going.

> That day was amazing. I learned so much. One thing was that when activists get tired — and I did — I should just remember what I am doing. We have to push for some of the big things we want despite little to show as achievements along the way. Ever since, I have been motivated to be more of a peace activist. I am glad I participated and I recommend that you take part in a march yourself. It's a blast!

Images of Peace
and Reconciliation

In the summer of 2001, I had the opportunity to attend a conference on university teaching and learning in Johannesburg, South Africa. We were fortunate to have one of my heroes for peace, Nelson Mandela, address our conference. Beaming and stately, he very graciously reminded us of our responsibility to help lead the world toward a peaceful and prosperous future. In a post-conference visit to Nepal and India, I heard directly about the conditions that were sparking conflicts in that region of the world.

In the summer of 2002, after my workshop, *Teaching and Learning Peace,* ended and after I completed a draft of this manuscript, I had the opportunity to attend a conference on university teaching in Vilnius, Lithuania and then travel to Warsaw, Krakow, Prague, and Budapest. I wanted to see first hand the legacy of World War II and the holocaust, to remind myself of the terrible price we pay when we neglect what is necessary for a sustainable peace.

A Polish band with traditional instruments plays Dixieland jazz on the streets of their reclaimed old town of Warsaw, Poland. Music has always been a bridge between cultures, promoting understanding and appreciation of differences. Much of Warsaw was reduced to rubble during World War II. It is a credit to the Polish people and their hopes for the future that they were able to emerge from war and restore some semblance of their rich architectural history.

Like democracy itself, peacemaking builds from a foundation of critical thinking and open dialogue about differences. Eula Papaandreu-Matusiak was active in organizing textile workers in New England with own my mother in the 1930s. Born in Portugal, she was later deported as a "national security threat" during the McCarthy era hysteria and persecutions of the 1950s. Although arrested many times during strikes, this sweet sprite was never convicted of any crime. Because Portugal was then a right wing dictatorship, however, Eula's return to her homeland would have put her at risk. Poland was quick to offer her asylum. She's well cared for but misses her friends in the U.S.

The Jewish ghetto in Krakow was largely emptied during the persecution by the Nazis, its residents murdered or worked to death in the nearby Auschwitz-Birkenau concentration camp. This area of Krakow was later used for filming some of Spielberg's *Schindler's List*. I have often used the section of the film that was shot here, when the Germans emptied the Jewish section, in my class on diversity in an attempt to convey some of the holocaust's terror. Our conversations about the dangers of intolerance take on a very different tone afterwards. Students seem much more clear about their responsibilities as future teachers when facing prejudice and discrimination.

Guards in elevated sentry boxes at Auschwitz-Birkenau often used inmates for target practice. Any education about peace must be included within military training. I remember meeting West German troops getting just such an orientation at Dachau years earlier.

Lithuanian churches were largely silent as local residents did the bidding of their Nazi overlords and persecuted their Jewish neighbors. Once a center for Jewish life and culture rivaling Warsaw and New York, the entire population of the Jewish ghetto here—100,000 men, women, and children—was systematically selected and slaughtered in the nearby Ponar forest. Just what was taught from the Lithuanian pulpits and during their Sunday school lessons? Churches can and must play a central role in building the foundation for a sustainable peace.

In Hungary, the Nazis continued their slaughter of Jews, gypsies, homosexuals, priests, union leaders—anyone who dissented —despite growing military losses on both fronts. Here at the synagogue in Budapest, an estimated 6,000 Jews are buried in a mass grave. For me, this tree symbolizes the affirmation of life that can, and must, arise from these horrors and point us all toward the forgiveness, reconciliation, and healing that will promote understanding and sustain peace.

In Prague, the 1968 uprising also sparked a Soviet military response although only a handful of Czechs died. What has been termed the *Velvet Revolution* then led to Czech independence as the Soviets, in the spirit of *Glasnost* (openness) under Gorbachev, renounced the use of force for sustaining alliances. There are important lessons in peacemaking here.

Our groundbreaking summer 2002 class on *Teaching and Learning Peace*. Teachers, professors, and graduate students joined with a minister, an eleven year old, self-styled peace activist, and concerned citizens to explore our roles as peacemakers.

References

Alberti, Robert. 1995. *Your perfect right: A guide to assertive living.* San Luis Obispo, CA: Impact.

Allport, Gordon. 1954. *The nature of prejudice.* Cambridge, MA: Addison-Wesley.

Armstrong, William. 1995. *Study is hard work.* Boston: Godine.

Belenky, Mary F., Blythe M. Clinchy, Nancy R. Goldberger, and Jill R. Tarule, eds. 1986. *Women's ways of knowing.* New York: Basic Books.

Berne, Eric. 1964. *Games people play. The psychology of human relations.* New York: Grove Press.

Berrigan, Daniel. 2000. Connecting the altar to the pentagon. In *Peace is the way,* ed. Walter Wink. New York: Maryknoll.

Bloom, Benjamin S. 1973. *Every kid can: Learning for mastery.* Washington, DC: College University Press.

Boal, Augusto. 1979. *Theater of the oppressed.* New York: Urizen.

Boal, Augusto. 1992. *Games for actors and non-actors.* New York: Routledge.

Boal, Augusto. 1995. *Rainbow of desire.* New York: Routledge.

Boulding, Elise. 2000. *Cultures of peace.* Syracuse, NY: Syracuse University Press.

Bouton, Clark, and B. Rice. 1983. Developing student skills and abilities. In *Learning in groups,* ed. Clark Bouton and Russell Garth. San Francisco: Jossey-Bass.

Brown, J. 1999. Lowdown on a high-strung corner of Europe. *The Christian Science Monitor* (March 16):12-13.

Bruinius, H. 1999. Plowed under: A tree no longer grows in Harlem. *The Christian Science Monitor* (March 12): 2, 4.

Bruner, Jerome. 1966. *Toward a theory of instruction.* Cambridge, MA: Harvard University Press.

Bruner, Jerome, J. Goodnow, and G. Austin. 1967. *A study of thinking.* New York: Science Editions.

Bry, Adelaide. 1973. *The TA primer: Transactional analysis in everyday life.* New York: Harper and Row.

Canter, Lee, and Marlene Canter. 1976. *Assertive discipline: A take-charge approach for today's educator.* Seal Beach, CA: Canter and Associates.

Chartier, Richard. 2000. Adolfo Perez Esquivel. In *Peace is the way,* edited by Walter Wink. New York: Maryknoll.

Christensen, C. Roland. 1982. Introduction. In *The art and craft of teaching,* ed. Margaret Gullette. Cambridge, MA: Harvard University Press.

Crum, Thomas. 1997. *Journey to center: Lessons in unifying body, mind, and spirit.* ?: Fireside.

Covey, Steven. 1989. *The seven habits of highly effective people.* New York: Simon and Schuster.

Davis, Barbara Gross. 1993. *Tools for teaching.* San Francisco: Jossey-Bass.

Dear, John. 2000. The experiments of Gandhi. In *Peace is the way,* ed. Walter Wink. New York: Maryknoll.

Deese, James, and Ellin Deese. 1994. *How to study.* New York: McGraw-Hill.

Dreikurs, Rudolf. 1968. *Psychology in the classroom: A manual for teachers.* New York: Harper and Row.

Eble, Kenneth. 1994. *The craft of teaching.* San Francisco: Jossey-Bass.

Erikson, Erik. 1974. *Dimensions of a new identity.* New York: Norton.

Ernst, Ken. 1973. *Games students play, and what to do about them.* Mellbrae, CA: Celestial Arts.

Farmer, James. 2000. The coming revolt against Jim Crow. In *Peace is the way,* ed. Walter Wink. New York: Maryknoll.

Finkel, D. and Monk, G. 1983. Teachers and learning groups: Dissolution of the Atlas complex. In *Learning in groups,* ed. Clark Bouton and Russell Garth. San Francisco: Jossey-Bass.

Forest, James. 2000. Remembering Dorothy Day. In *Peace is the way,* ed. Walter Wink. New York: Maryknoll.

Fox, R., Boies, H., Brainard, L., Fletcher, E., Huge, J., Logan, C., Schmuck, R., Shaheen, T., and Stegeman, W. 1974. *School climate improvement: A challenge to the school administrator.* Bloomington, IN: Phi Delta Kappa.

Freed, Alvyn. 1971. *TA for kids (and grown-ups, too).* Sacramento: Jalmar Press.

Freed, Alvyn. 1973. *TA for teens (and other important people).* Sacramento: Jalmar Press.

Freire, Paulo. 1970. *Pedagogy of the oppressed.* New York: Seabury.

Friedman, Maurice. 2000. Hasidism and the love of enemies. In *Peace is the way,* ed. Walter Wink. New York: Maryknoll.

Firesen, Dorothy. 2000. Social action and the need for prayer. In *Peace is the way,* ed. Walter Wink. New York: Maryknoll.

Gagne, Robert. 1985. *The conditions of learning and theory of instruction.* 4th ed. New York: Holt, Rinehart and Winston.

Gardner, Howard. 1983. *Frames of mind.* New York: Basic Books.

Gardner, Howard. 1999a. *The disciplined mind: What all students should understand.* New York: Simon and Schuster.

Gardner, Howard. 199b. *Intelligence reframed: Multiple intelligences for the 21st century.* New York: Basic Books.

Gardner, John, and A. Jerome Jewler. 1997. *Your college experience.* New York: Wadsworth.

Gilligan, Carol. 1982. *In a different voice: Psychological theory and woman's development.* Cambridge, MA: Harvard University Press.

Gilligan, Carol, Annie Rogers, and Deborah Tulman, eds. 1991. *Women, girls, and psychotherapy: Reframing resistance.* New York: Harrington Park Press.

Glasser, William. 1969. *Schools without failure.* New York: Harper and Row.

Glasser, William. 1975. *Reality therapy.* New York: Harper and Row.

Glasser, William. 1986. *Control theory in the classroom.* New York: Harper and Row.

Glasser, William. 1992. *The quality school: Managing students without coercion.* New York: Harper-Collins.

Goleman, Daniel. 1994. *Emotional intelligence.* New York: Bantam.

Goodale, G. 1999. How they imagined 'Shakespeare in Love.' *The Christian Science Monitor* (March 5):17.

Gordon, Thomas. 1974. *Teacher effectiveness training.* New York: Peter H. Whyden.

Goss-Mayr, Hildegard. 2000. When prayer and revolution become people power. In *Peace is the way,* ed. Walter Wink. New York: Maryknoll.

Gregorc, Anthony. 1982. *An adult's guide to style.* Columbia, CT: Gregorc.

Hanh, Thich Nhat. 1991. *Peace is the way.* New York: Bantam.

Hanh, Thich Nhat. 2000. Being peace. In *Peace is the way,* ed. Walter Wink. New York: Maryknoll.

Harding, Vincent. 2000. We must keep going: Martin Luther King Jr. and the future of America. In *Peace is the way,* ed. Walter Wink. New York: Maryknoll.

Harris, Thomas. 1969. *I'm OK — you're OK: A practical guide to transactional analysis.* New York: Harper and Row.

Hawken, Paul. 1993. *The ecology of commerce.* New York: HarperCollins.

Hawley, R. 1974. *Value exploration through role playing.* Amherst, MA: ERA Press.

Holdridge, S. 2000. The precautionary principle. *Timeline,* (May/June):, 14-17.

Johnson, David, and Roger Johnson. 1994. *Learning together and alone.* Needham Heights, MA: Allyn and Bacon.

Johnson, David, Roger Johnson, and Kurt Smith. 1989. *Cooperative learning: Cooperation and competition, theory, and research,* Edina, MN: Interaction Book Co.

Joyce, Bruce, Marsha Weil, and Emily Calhoun. 2000. *Models of Teaching.* Englewood Cliffs, NJ: Prentice-Hall.

King, Martin Luther, Jr. 2000. Facing the challenge of a new age. In *Peace is the way,* ed. Walter Wink. New York: Maryknoll.

King, Martin Luther, Jr. 2000. My pilgrimage to nonviolence. In *Peace is the way,* ed. Walter Wink. New York: Maryknoll.

Kohlberg, Lawrence. 1963. The development of children's orientation toward moral order: Sequence in the development of moral thought. *Vita Humana* 6: 11-33.

Kohlberg, Lawrence. 1981. *The philosophy of moral development: Moral stages and the ideal of justice.* New York: Harper and Row.

Kuhn, Thomas. 1970. *The structure of scientific revolutions.* Chicago: University of Chicago Press.

Levine, Arthur, and Jeanette Cureton. 1998. *When hope and fear collide.* San Francisco: Jossey-Bass.

Levinson, Daniel. 1978. *The seasons of a man's life.* New York: Ballentine.

Levinson, Daniel, and Judy Levinson. 1996. *The seasons of a woman's life.* New York: Random House.

Lezotte, L., D. Hathaway, S. Miller, J. Passalacqua, and W. Brookover. 1980. *School learning climate and school achievement.* Tallahassee, FL: The Site Specific Technical Assistance Center.

Light, R. 1992. *The Harvard assessment seminars.* Cambridge, MA: Harvard University's Graduate School of Education and Kennedy School of Government.

Limerick, Patricia. 2000. *Something in the soil,* New York: Norton.

Longman, D. and R. Atkinson. 1999. *College learning and study skills.* New York: Wadsworth.

Lowman, Joseph. 1995. *Mastering the techniques of teaching.* San Francisco: Jossey-Bass.

Maguire, Mairead. 2000. Gandhi and the ancient wisdom of nonviolence. In *Peace is the way,* ed. Walter Wink. New York: Maryknoll.

Maimon, E. 1983. Graduate education and cooperative scholarship. In *Learning in groups,* ed. Clark Bouton and Russell Garth. San Francisco: Jossey-Bass.

Maslow, Abraham. 1959. *New knowledge in human values.* New York: Harper & Row.

Mandela, Nelson. 1994. *Long walk to freedom.* Boston: Little Brown.

McClelland, David. 1985. *Human motivation.* Glenville, IL: Scott Foresman.

McKeachie, Wibert J., et al. 2002. *McKeachie's teaching tips.* St. Charles, IL: Houghton Mifflin.

Michaelsen, Larry K. 1983. Team learning in large classes. In *Learning in groups,* ed. Clark Bouton and Russell Garth. San Francisco: Jossey-Bass.

Moberg, D. 1999. The good doctor: Samuel Epstein seeks a second opinion on the causes of cancer. *Utne Reade* (March-April): 22-23.

Nouwen, Henri. 2000. Saying no to death. In *Peace is the way,* ed. Walter Wink. New York: Maryknoll.

Orr, David. 1994. *Earth in mind: On education, environment, and the human prospect.* Washington, DC: Island Press.

Palmer, Parker. 1998. *The courage to teach.* San Francisco: Jossey-Bass

Patrick, C. 1955. *What is creative thinking.* New York: Philosophica Library.

Perry, William. 1999. *Forms of intellectual and ethical development in the college years.* San Francisco: Jossey-Bass.

Piaget, Jerome. 1952. *The origins of intelligence in children.* Translated by M. Cook. New York: International Universities Press.

Ramsden, Paul. 1992. *Learning to teach in higher education.* London: Routledge.

Rogoff, Barbara. 1990. *Apprenticeship in thinking.* New York: Oxford University Press.

Rowe, M. 1974. Wait time and rewards as instructional variables: Their influence on language, logic and fate control. Part 1: Wait-time. *Journal of Research in Science Teaching* 11: 81-94.

Sarasin, Lynne Celli. 1998. *Learning style perspectives: Impact in the classroom.* Madison, WI: Atwood Publishing.

Shaheen, R., and Pedrick, W. 1974. *School district climate improvement.* Denver: CFK Limited.

Sheehy, Gail. 1974. *Passages: Predictable crises of adult life.* New York: E. P. Dutton.

Simon, Sidney, Leslie Howe, and Howard Kirschenbaum. 1972. *Values clarification: A handbook of practical strategies for teachers and students.* New York: Hart.

Simon, Sidney, and J. Clark. 1975. *More values clarification: Strategies for the classroom.* San Diego: Pennant.

Skinner, B.F. 1953. *Science and human behavior.* New York: Macmillan.

Solnit, Rebecca. 1994. *Savage dreams: A journey into the landscape wars of the American West.* New York: Vintage.

Sperling, Godfrey. 1999. Gore's Clinton problem. *The Christian Science Monitor,* March 16, 11.

Suchman, J. 1962. The elementary school training program in scientific inquiry. *Report to the U.S. Office of Education, Project Title VII.* Urbana: University of Illinois.

Takaki, Ronald. 1993. *A different mirror.* Boston: Little Brown.

Tharp, Roland, and Ronald Gallimore. 1988. *Rousing minds to life.* NY: Cambridge University Press.

Timpson, Anne Burlack. 2002. Unpublished autobiographical manuscript.

Timpson, William M., and Paul Bendel-Simso. 1996. *Concepts and choices for teaching.* Madison, WI: Atwood Publishing.

Timpson, William M., and F. Broadbent, eds. 1995. *Action learning: Experiences and promise.* Brisbane, Australia: Tertiary Education Institute, University of Queensland.

Timpson, William M., and Suzanne Burgoyne. 2002. *Teaching and performing.* Madison, WI: Atwood Publishing.

Timpson, William M., and David N. Tobin. 1982. *Teaching as performing.* Englewood Cliffs, NJ: Prentice-Hall.

Timpson, William M. 1988. Paulo Freire: Advocate of literacy through liberation. *Educational Leadership* 45: 62-66.

Timpson, William M. 1999. *Metateaching and the instructional map.* Madison, WI: Atwood Publishing.Timpson, William M. 1999. *Metateaching and the instructional map.* Madison, WI: Atwood Publishing.

Timpson, William M. 2001. *Stepping up: College learning and community for a sustainable future.* Madison, WI: Atwood Publishing/Cincinnati, OH: Thomson Learning.

Tobias, Sheila. 1992. *They're not dumb, they're different.* Tucson, AZ: Research Corporation.

von Oech, Roger. 1983. *A whack on the side of the head.* New York: Warner.

von Oech, Roger. 1986. *A kick in the seat of the pants.* New York: Warner.

Walter, Timothy, and Al Siebert. 1996. *How to succeed in college.* New York: Harcourt Brace.

Wolfgang, Charles. 1995. *Solving discipline problems.* Boston: Allyn and Bacon.

INDEX